SPATIALIZING
JUSTICE

SPATIALIZING JUSTICE

BUILDING BLOCKS

TEDDY CRUZ AND FONNA FORMAN

Hatje Cantz Verlag

The MIT Press
Cambridge, Massachusetts

Return the Body to Democracy 7
For Michael Sorkin

Building Blocks: An Introduction 13

BUILDING BLOCKS 18

01 CONFRONT INEQUALITY
02 CONSTRUCT THE POLITICAL
03 RECUPERATE INSTITUTIONAL MEMORY
04 DECOLONIZE KNOWLEDGE
05 RADICALIZE THE LOCAL
06 VISUALIZE URBAN CONFLICT
07 TRANSGRESS BORDERS
08 REIMAGINE JURISDICTION
09 COMPLICATE AUTONOMY
10 TEMPORALIZE INFRASTRUCTURE
11 TRANSLATE THE INFORMAL
12 PERFORM CITIZENSHIP
13 SOCIALIZE DENSITY
14 RETHINK OWNERSHIP
15 RESIST PRIVATIZATION
16 DEMAND GENERATIVE ZONING
17 MOBILIZE NEIGHBORHOODS AS POLITICAL UNITS
18 VALIDATE EVERYDAY WORK
19 INTERVENE IN THE DEVELOPER'S PROFORMA
20 CO-DEVELOP WITH COMMUNITIES
21 TRANSFORM HOUSING BEYOND "UNITS"
22 TRANSCEND HOSPITALITY
23 DEMOCRATIZE ACCESS
24 ACTIVATE PUBLIC SPACE
25 CURATE NEW URBAN PEDAGOGIES
26 CIVICIZE PLATFORMS
27 DESIGN MEDIATION
28 TALK TO THE ~~ENEMY~~ ADVERSARY
29 PROBLEMATIZE "SUSTAINABILITY"
30 RETOOL OURSELVES

Notes 143
Colophon 144

Return the Body to Democracy
For Michael Sorkin

During the worst pandemic in a century, American society is divided between those who wear masks and those who don't, between those eager to be vaccinated and those who refuse. The dissolution of social reciprocity, the collision between collective commitment and rugged individualism, between public and private, remain the single greatest obstacle to healing our society and rebuilding more equitable and inclusive cities as we slowly emerge from this pandemic. And climate change is coming. COVID-19 was the canary in the coalmine, like the universe testing us to get our priorities straight.

We lost our friend Michael Sorkin in the earliest days of the pandemic. We hear every day about viral mutations, and we wonder: can the virus—this virus that took Michael—mutate into an unexpected antidote to selfishness? Can this moment expose the collective costs of austerity, of eroding the social safety net, of neglecting public challenges like racism, climate disruption, deepening inequality, and surging nationalism everywhere?

In 1997 Michael was invited to deliver the Raoul Wallenberg Lecture at the University of Michigan. Wallenberg was a Swedish diplomat and architect who saved thousands of Jews in German-occupied Hungary during the later stages of World War II. Honoring this humanitarian architect and trafficker of people in an undemocratic state, Michael called his talk *Traffic in Democracy*.[1] A powerful reflection on the afflictions of urban democracy, the piece transcends decades, Michael's voice lampooning the idiocy and injustices of rapidly ascending late 20th century neoliberal life in America—and yet it is astonishingly germane to this moment.

Michael's narrative centered on the idea of propinquity, a concept that he and Joan Copjec explored further in their 1999 collection, *Giving Ground: The Politics of Propinquity*.[2] For Michael "being together physically," bodies in space, was essential to the practice of deliberative democracy—and it was radically opposed to the American version of democracy, born on the frontier, understood as the right to be left alone. Michael valued an urbanity of propinquity—equitable linkages, connections, flows and exchanges, where freedom is a collective and civic concept—active, positive, participatory. At bottom, propinquity summarized Michael's determination to coexist with others in urban space. We cannot possibly imagine freedom, he wrote, outside of a structure of interaction with others. "City air makes people free."

Propinquity was an illuminating concept to us back then, and we wondered how we had ever lived without it. And now, with Michael gone, we feel we have never in our lifetimes needed this concept more. Democracy demands cities designed for propinquity. Michael loved the Athenian agora, a funky urban space that "supported both efficient passage and organized encounters while simultaneously offering innumerable routes and circulamsances for chance, unstructured, accidental and serendipitous encounters—so intrinsic to the working of democracy." He might as well have been describing his beloved New York City—a perpetually unstable "juxtaposition engine," as he called it.

But Michael worried that propinquity was under attack by a variety of forces, some remarkably relevant to our moment. One was the systematic fragmentation of the public, a function of both fashionable communitarian erosion from within as well as privatization from without. He worried that identitarian entrenchment fragmented the public into multiple publics vying for recognition, that it undermined collective resistance to the forces of privatization encroaching into our public spaces. Communitarianism also unwittingly fueled strategies to market architecture as a bridge to fixed identities—and that typically ends up dispossessing and gentrifying urban neighborhoods.

He never imagined the virtual world we now inhabit; but even in its nascence Michael saw the internet as a menacing threat to democracy. While proponents were heralding the possibilities of instantaneous and free global communication, and no doubt there were emancipatory examples around the world, Michael worried about reinventing proximity through virtual encounter, and saw little value, for example, in virtual town halls, which he described as a passive "spectacle of someone else being heard."

For Michael, democracy demands participation reliably "in the open." In *Traffic in Democracy*, he asked: "What happens when neither wealth nor information nor happiness is exchanged face to face, when communication increasingly takes place by dissolving the space of action?"

Michael's was an urbanity of the body. "If the body ever ceases to be the privileged means of participation in and enjoyment of urban life," he wrote, "urban life is at an end." For him the answer to a bodiless body politic, to anti-public, anti-collective, consumerized, gated and themed idiocy was always *to return the body to democracy.* This is the driving theme of his Wallenberg lecture. And we have no doubt this would be his response today. *Return the body to democracy.* And for Michael, the neighborhood is always the urban increment. A space of face-to-face deliberation among bodies in real time, neighborhoods are the logical scale for local democracy and environmental accountability. Neighborhoods harmonize the speed of the market and slowness of the civic, the private and the public. And they challenge the frontier mentality of growth understood as an unlimited horizon to manipulate value at the edges. Michael's radicalization of urban ecology was like Jane Jacobs on green steroids—but stained with a little bit of red—reminding us that greening the city without social priorities is just decoration and a feel-good response to environmental crisis.

What a moment he left us in. He might tell us now that the virus which took him might be the strange harbinger of something better, exposing the stupidity of selfishness during a collective crisis, the catastrophe of freedom-thinking, of isolationism, of disinvestment from public goods, and the eroding of public commitment.

Maybe this moment can instigate a paradigm shift in our public priorities once we bodily reunite? Can we envision the end of capitalist greed? The reemergence of a progressive welfare state? A commitment to more equitable and sustainable cities? The reorganization of institutions to confront racial injustice?

Our entrance into the third decade of the 21ˢᵗ century has been a wake-up call of our radical interdependence, our need for truth, transparency, social trust, and planetary coordination. Perhaps from all this, a renewed public consciousness might be born, reminding us that the survival of the individual depends on the health of the collective.

And yet, Michael worried that architects were dropping the ball. He believed they needed to engage this reconstruction of common ground. He closed *Traffic in Democracy* with bucket of cold water. If you like what I am saying here, why in practice are you all so damned complicit? Why have you embraced a politics of disengagement, abandoning the field to the avatars of bigness and smallness who have in common the production of sameness? We've become phobic, he said, to thinking of cities as physical as well as social constructions. And we suffer from a tremendous poverty of both vision and will. And the dominant models are unsatisfactory, consisting of "go-with-the-flow neo-suburbanism, fingers-crossed laissez-faire, tepid riffs on the garden city, retreaded modernism, and Disneyland."

He insisted we scrutinize our clichés and platitudes as urbanists and architects, our banal ways of practicing. And he inspired an entire generation, us included, to reflect critically on our own practices. WHY do we do WHAT we do? For WHOM? WHERE? WHEN? and HOW? He thought, taught, wrote, and practiced by example.

Michael's urban fantasies over decades, made of strange organic architectural shapes, unfolding seamlessly within social and ecological systems, threading public space, mobility and housing as integrated social scaffolds were both anarchic and unyieldingly civic. They manifested a commitment to progressive governance and the agency of bottom-up self-organization and civic participation. Michael's writings, sketches, and the echo of his words will always remind us of our radical interdependence.

Michael believed architects can be political agents, taking a position against what is morally and ethically wrong. His memory is heavy with the traces he left us. So let's carry forward his infectious optimism for a better world, his childish energy and wicked humor lifting up the potential of everything from the rubble of conflict, injustice, alienation and pandemic.

Michael will remain the social and political consciousness of the architectural field. Our work dwells within the spirit of this legacy, and we dedicate this book to him.

Teddy Cruz and Fonna Forman
San Diego/Tijuana, 2022

We live just a few miles from the child detention centers that will forever stain this period of American history. The San Diego-Tijuana border zone is a geography of vivid contrasts and a microcosm of planetary crises: political violence, dramatic inequality and labor exploitation, fragmented social ecologies, the disproportionate impacts of climate disruption, unprecedented human displacement and migration across geopolitical borders. This zone also localizes the hegemony of neoliberal urbanization across the world, and the devastation it wreaks on collective economic, social and natural resources. The proximities of wealth and extreme poverty in this uneven region are staggering.

Remaining neutral in the face of these injustices makes one complicit. Working here over the last decades, we have questioned the role of architects and urban designers to confront the crises of our time. Engaging this unique territory of urgent challenges as a global laboratory has meant rethinking our approach to research and design, and repositioning ourselves.

Our research-based practice, *Estudio Teddy Cruz + Fonna Forman*, is an unconventional partnership between a political theorist and an architect. Merging research, practice and pedagogy, our office is based inside a public research university, the University of California, San Diego. Against the dystopic backdrop of the border region—and risking professional suicide as architects—we came to understand that spatializing justice demands not only a focus on buildings, but a fundamental reorganization of social and economic relations. We concluded at some point that exposing the drivers of inequality and challenging exclusionary urban policies that undermine spatial justice is a generative ground for a more experimental architecture. We believe that a new political economy of urbanization, and a new design intelligence, can emerge from within peripheral zones of regional contestation like ours (and that transformational creativity is less likely to arise from within sites of stability and economic power). We believe that a new generation of architects and urban designers can anticipate new ways of thinking and doing, demand a new collective imagination with spatial implications, and steward a reorganization of public priorities and investment.

Anticipating new ways of thinking and doing means confronting the clichés of our creative fields and rethinking who we serve, expanding our range to contact domains that have remained peripheral to design, and cultivating a new kind of collective advocacy that transforms architecture into a social medium capable of challenging urban norms and spatializing public commitments.

We have learned a great deal about spatializing justice studying Latin America lineages of participatory urbanization over the last decades. In our lab we research municipalities that have "co-produced" the city from the bottom-up, from Porto Alegre and Curitiba, Brazil to Bogotá and Medellín, Colombia. We have been documenting these cases in close collaboration and dialogue with the key political and civic actors who led them. These cities have taught us that urban transformation must begin with social transformation—and that design has an essential role to play. We believe that architects and urban designers can be facilitators of a new civic conversation, interlocutors of institutional memory, orchestrators of renewed public priorities, curators of inclusive civic programming, and designers of fresh formal and aesthetic categories that problematize dominant neoliberal agendas in the city that manipulate and monetize relations between the social and the spatial. We can design cultural interventions that expose the lie of trickle-down economics, that uproot anti-democratic myths that sow cynicism about progressive governance, undermine public culture and lead the electorate astray. Architects and urban designers can help reinvigorate a basic social contract that anchors individual well-being in collective well-being.

Reinterpreting architecture as a social medium capable of changing hearts and minds, and reorienting urbanization, begins by critically engaging the conditions that have produced our urban crises. These conditions become the material for design. Mobilizing urban conflict as a catalyst for design means exposing the controversies and contradictions inscribed in a particular socio-spatial condition, the exclusionary policies and the hidden histories of oppression. These critical investigations motivate a sense of urgency, and help to orient thinking and practical design methods. In our case, these critical investigations typically confirm our intuition that the first site of intervention is not a physical site, but a strategic detour from architecture into sedimented institutional protocols, harmful social norms, discriminatory financialization practices, the war between public and private interests, or the gap between top-down resources and bottom-up urban creativity. Traveling at the edges of the architecture field demands epistemic humility and openness to new worlds of knowledge and practice. Our aspiration is to partner with diverse urban actors to co-produce new knowledges and strategies, and to co-design civic and political processes that prioritize social, racial and environmental justice, urban pedagogies that render the complexity of contested urban dynamics more accessible to diverse publics, and new economic collaborations among conventionally divided sectors to share the responsibility of public works.

In other words, we seek to design and fertilize a new political ground, new civic languages, from which new infrastructures for inclusion can emerge. In our practice, the design of physical projects is always linked with the design of processes, protocols and programs that aim to civicize and democratize the spaces, knowledges and resources of the city.

This current period, marked by global pandemic, social rupture, institutional polarization and paralysis, the corrosion of democratic commitments, and innumerable crises across all imaginable registers, epistemic, social, economic, environmental and political, has culminated in what we perceive as a *crisis of the public*: a failure to tackle collectively the most urgent issues impacting our shared destiny. Given the planetary challenges we face in these early years of the twenty-first century, remaining socially relevant as architects and urban designers requires transforming our own design practices as critical sites of intervention, retooling ourselves, refreshing our approaches through new criteria, new clients, new briefs, new sites, new strategies of advocacy, and a new imperative to close the gap between artistic experimentation and social responsibility, the aspirations of the historic *avant-garde* in design.

The moment seemed right for us to pause, to reflect on our own practice, and assemble key commitments—what we call "Building Blocks" —that have grounded our research-based practice over the last decades. We identified thirty of them and while we hesitate to characterize them as a manifesto, they are organized thematically as tight, impressionistic statements, manifesto-like in their brevity. While they have been generative for us, orienting our visualization projects, urban and architectural interventions, writing, exhibitions and pedagogies, we hope they might be useful to other designers and spatial practices as they reposition themselves in this evolving reality, to students who aspire to socially relevant, public-interest work, and to design educators who bear primary responsibility for nurturing the aspirations of a new generation and reorienting design education. Ultimately, we hope the Building Blocks will provoke conversation about the role of architects and designers in this next period of urbanization.

The arc of our work over the last years—our priorities and projects both physical and programmatic—is presented in two volumes, both co-published by Hatje Cantz Verlag and the MIT Press. The current volume, *Spatializing Justice: Building Blocks*, is the first and outlines the commitments of our embedded research-based practice at the US-Mexico border. The second volume, *Socializing Architecture: Top-Down/ Bottom-Up*, assembles key writings, exhibitions, and twenty-two concrete projects and initiatives that manifest these commitments.

The Building Blocks position justice as a spatial concept, conceived dialectically as bottom-up urban power that recognizes, resists and counters the harms, degradations and exploitations of exclusionary top-down power—discriminatory urban regulation, the rule of law, and the entrenched conventions, social norms and biases that sustain these institutions. In other words, we articulate justice as a collective power from below to reclaim the city as a democratic and inclusive field. We believe that design can mediate conflicts between law and urban justice, between the top-down and the bottom-up, to spatialize collective rights to the city.

Each Building Block occupies two spreads across four pages and contains three elements: a *Provocation*, a *Referent*, and the *Building Block* itself. The first page begins with a *Provocation* that describes an urban problematic that demands coordinated action from below. It is intended to provoke imaginative strategies to transcend it. The second page continues with a *Referent,* a brief description of an empirical case study, a story or an anecdote, a historical or contemporary example. Sometimes the Referent is a systemic failure, sometimes an untapped opportunity, sometimes a brilliant example of success, sometimes an unrequited urban fantasy. Spread across the third and fourth pages is the *Building Block* itself, which performs as an operational diagram for action. Sometimes the Building Block elaborates a process from within our design practice; sometimes it contains a speculative pathway, or translates an anecdote of bottom-up praxis through which we extrapolate a set of procedures. The Building Block is always visualized through a table or a process-based diagram that prioritizes concepts and prompts new ways of thinking and doing. It demonstrates our belief that diagrams are not merely descriptive devices for visualizing data, but projective tools that perform the information they contain and anticipate a course of action. In this sense, the Building Blocks are strategies for social, institutional and spatial transformation.

Obviously transformative processes require specificity, detail and trust that can only happen in the flows of real life. The Building Blocks are meant to provoke imaginative thinking about what a provocation would look like in a specific context familiar to the reader. In fact, we have been critical of academic narratives about urban justice that remain conjectural and abstract, far removed from the lived experiences of people in the world. Even admirable progressive agendas for spatializing justice often dwell in symbolic terrain, lacking concrete pathways for social, institutional and spatial transformation. We hear regularly: "there is a housing crisis, and we need more *affordability*! there is a climate crisis, and we need more *resilience*!" But to make any progress at all, each of these pleas requires a shift from abstraction to specificity, a detailed working program with civic, institutional and spatial strategies: a new conversation with new voices; alterations in public perceptions and priorities; a constellation of committed institutional actors and communities; top-down and bottom-up shifts in municipal processes, decision-making and policy; and a rearrangement of urban spatial hierarchies to support inclusion.

A Building Block is a point of entry, an opening, a Socratic irritant, that provokes the questions we must ask if we want different answers, and the actions we must take if we want different outcomes. These provocations have emerged for us while working in a particular zone of conflict at the US-Mexico border. In this sense, perhaps our most important Building Block is to *Radicalize the Local*, to demystify place as provincial and nativist, and to elevate the local as the unit of analysis and action. We seek a "critical proximity" with global conflicts that hit the ground in our immediate context and the particular communities entangled in them. In this sense, the Building Blocks represent local processes for global urbanizations of justice.

BUILDING BLOCKS

01 CONFRONT INEQUALITY

Inequality is the Summoner

Where is Our Battle Diagram?

Naming the Drivers of Inequality

02 CONSTRUCT THE POLITICAL

Neutrality is Complicity

Return Duchamp's Urinal to the Bathroom!

A Map of Detours

03 RECUPERATE INSTITUTIONAL MEMORY

Where is the New Deal?

American Dream Nightmare?

Saez-Piketty Redux

04 DECOLONIZE KNOWLEDGE

Visualizing Urban Histories of Racial Injustice

Cumulative Impacts of Racism, Redlining, Disinvestment and Climate Change

Epistemic Justice in Design: Co-producing Knowledge

05 RADICALIZE THE LOCAL

From Ambiguity to Specificity

A Critical Proximity

Mandala of Local Power

06 VISUALIZE URBAN CONFLICT

Urban Conflict is Our Creative Tool

Architectures of Dissensus

60 Linear Miles of Urban Conflict

07 TRANSGRESS BORDERS

The Wall Exists Only to be Transgressed

Chronology of an Invasion

Deborder: Urbanizations Beyond the Property Line

08 REIMAGINE JURISDICTION

The Conflict Between the Natural and the Political

Dumb Sovereignty: Nation Against Nature

Micro-Basins as Neighborhoods

09 COMPLICATE AUTONOMY

Challenging Self-Referentiality

Autonomy and the Metropolitan Battlefield

Relational Architectures

10 TEMPORALIZE INFRASTRUCTURE

Infrastructure is a Verb

The Instant Market

Socializing Infrastructural Urbanism

11 TRANSLATE THE INFORMAL

The Informal as Praxis

Scaffolds for Things to Happen

Informal Algorithms

12 PERFORM CITIZENSHIP

Immigrant Civitas

Citizen-Architects

Mapping "Nonconformity"

13 SOCIALIZE DENSITY

Recalculating Density

Challenging Selfish Sprawl: McMansion Retrofitted

Density = # of Social Exchanges per Area

14 RETHINK OWNERSHIP

Challenging the "Ownership Society"

Retooling Co-ownership

Owning the Means of Production

15 RESIST PRIVATIZATION

Reject the Privatization of Everything

The Democratization of Surplus Value

Designing New Social-Economic Coalitions

16 DEMAND GENERATIVE ZONING

The Apartheid of Everyday Life

Visual Prompts for an Anticipatory Zoning

Piercing Blanket Zoning

17 MOBILIZE NEIGHBOR-HOODS AS POLITICAL UNITS

From Cities of Consumption to Neighborhoods of Production

The Snail Garden: A Cooperative at the Scale of the Block

"Bundling" Bottom-Up Practices

18 VALIDATE EVERYDAY WORK

Restoring the Social Value of Labor

Feminist Architectures

Re-collectivizing the Kitchen

19 INTERVENE IN THE DEVELOPER'S PROFORMA

Appropriating the Knowledge of the Developer

Activating the Hidden Value of "Sweat Equity"

Socializing the Developer's Proforma: Bundling Sweat Equity

20 CO-DEVELOP WITH COMMUNITIES

Developing the City with "Others"

What Do We Do While Waiting for the Urban Revolution to Arrive?

Protocols for Shared Urbanization

21 TRANSFORM HOUSING BEYOND "UNITS"

In Conditions of Poverty, "Units" Cannot Exist on Their Own

Pruitt-Igoe was Not Evil

Embedding Social Housing in Infrastructures of Support

22 TRANSCEND HOSPITALITY

From Hospitality to Inclusion

The Right to Migrate, the Right to Remain, the Right to Return

From Ephemeral Habitation to Incremental Permanency

23 DEMOCRATIZE ACCESS

Unwalling Space

She Sat Where She Did Not Belong

Designing the Rights of Entry

24 ACTIVATE PUBLIC SPACE

Public Space Constructs Citizen Culture

Spatializing Citizenship in Medellín

Designing Spaces and Protocols Together

25 CURATE NEW URBAN PEDAGOGIES

Increasing Public Knowledge: Problematizing Advocacy Planning

Bogotá's "Citizenship Cards"

Designing Community Processes

26 CIVICIZE PLATFORMS

Challenging the Algorithmic Regime

The Tragedy of the Commons Redux

Reclaiming the Digital Commons

27 DESIGN MEDIATION

Designing Interface

It is Not about "What" We Represent, but "Who" We Represent

Designing Mediation

28 TALK TO THE ~~ENEMY~~ ADVERSARY

Enough Preaching to the Choir

Border-Drain-Crossing

An Architecture of Dialogue

29 PROBLEMATIZE "SUSTAINABILITY"

Sustainability Begins with Civically Engaged Publics

Sustainable Hummer?

Bending the Curve

30 RETOOL OURSELVES

Intervening in Our Own Practices

Diagramming Practice: 5Ws + HOW

The Practice Diagram

Confront Inequality

Inequality is the Summoner

The celebrated economic boom and metropolitan growth of recent decades have produced dramatic inequality and uneven urban development, with an explosion of slums and marginalized neighborhoods surrounding major urban centers across the world. At bottom, inequality is an institutional attack on human dignity, supported by social norms and deployed through deliberate economic agendas that spatialize segregation, racism and exclusion. Urban violence is a direct consequence of disinvestment and neglect. How can our design fields collectively confront urban asymmetry? All urban and architectural initiatives today must begin by confronting the institutional mechanisms that exacerbate social and economic disparity. Inequality is the axis around which our political stance as designers should be reorganized.

01

Where is Our Battle Diagram?

Some contemporary architects working with morpho-genetic, computational design have declared that the goal of parametric architecture is to give aesthetic order to the visual messiness of the neoliberal city. The suggestion that the neoliberal city is an object that needs to be unified stylistically ignores the actual havoc that market fundamentalism has inflicted on the contemporary city during the last decades of economic boom—and that this havoc is not just a visual phenomenon but a set of deliberate choices to damage our collective, economic and natural resources. Many designers have also conveyed that it is not our responsibility as designers to resolve social and economic inequality and uneven urban development. We understand the limitations of any specialized field, but in the last 100 years, the most compelling *avant-garde* movements in architecture have always engaged pressing societal issues and their formal and aesthetic consequences—from Le Corbusier's foundational CIAM battle diagram that rallied its members to engage urgent social housing issues, to Constant's search for an architecture organized around socio-spatial contingencies.

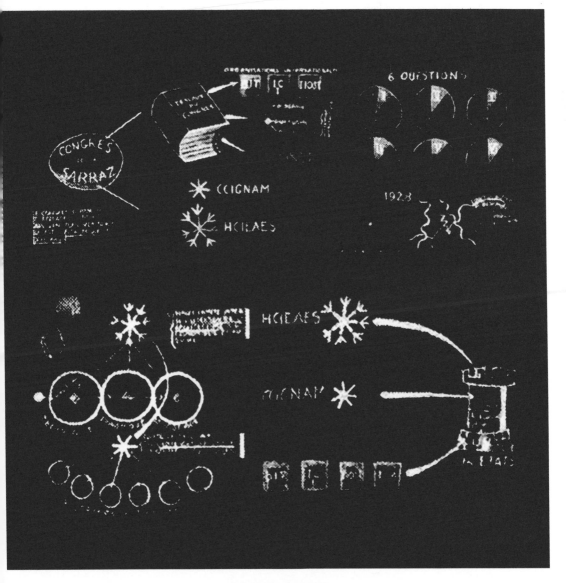

The Erosion of the Safety Net

The COVID-19 crisis exposed the social and economic costs of austerity. It is abundantly clear that since the ascendance of neoliberalism in the 1980s, public cuts in education, health and social services have widened the gap between rich and poor.

Invest in the poor, repair social infrastructure! ●

Unchecked Privatization

Anti-government ideology prompted a massive shift from public to private management logics: the privatization of everything became the mantra of economic progress. The privatization of collective assets deepened inequality.

Don't privatize; restructure the public! ◉

Deregulation

The negative impact of deregulation was emblematized by the banking crisis of 2008, exposing what can happen in the absence of regulatory frameworks for the protection of public assets, and the dangers of institutional unaccountability.

Demand institutional accountability! O

Defunding of Public Works

When privatization increases, public investment in infrastructure decreases and the gap between rich and poor widens. There is a direct correlation between disinvestment from infrastructure and an increase in poverty, social disparity and exclusion.

Invest in public infrastructure; broaden its social meaning! □

Dissolution of Labor Unions

In the United States today, unions have less presence than they did decades ago. With unions playing a smaller economic role, the gap between worker and CEO pay is 10 times greater today than it was in 1980.

Rebuild labor unions to protect workers! ✕

Tax Cuts to the Wealthy

Challenging the mythology of trickle-down economics, progressive taxation, which take a larger percentage of income from high-income earners, always narrows income gaps between the rich and everyone else. In recent decades the American tax system has done no such narrowing. In fact, it has widened the gap by cutting taxes on corporations and mega-wealth.

Progressive taxation is a civic duty! +

Inverse Relation Between Productivity and Compensation

Productivity has increased at a relatively consistent rate since 1948. But since the 1970s, the wages of American workers have not kept pace. While worker productivity has increased 132.8% during recent decades, their wages have remained stagnant.

Raise the minimum wage! ∧

Racism and Segregation

Redlining and exclusionary zoning racialize and spatialize poverty by design, deepening the wealth divide in the United States. At the close of the 20th century the average white family had a net worth six times greater than the average black family. This gap has now doubled. The wealth gap between white and Hispanic households has widened as well.

Dismantle structural racism! ∨

Concentration of Economic and Political Power

As of 2020, 0.1% of Americans had nearly 200 times more wealth than everyone else. These same mega-wealthy people have hijacked political power. The "Citizens United" Supreme Court decision legitimized unlimited political spending, and solidified elite influence over political opinion.

Democratize wealth and political power! /

Housing Unaffordability

Nearly 50% of Americans during the COVID-19 crisis were either poor or low-income—the highest rate in almost 60 years—and millions of Americans are struggling to afford a place to live, spending on average 48% of their income on housing and transportation.

Affordable housing is a right! ＼

Voter Supression

The deep structural barriers that have always made voting more difficult for people of color than for their white counterparts continue to deepen in 2021 through voter suppression laws, further eroding the 1965 Voting Rights Act.

Get out the vote! —

Uneven Political Representation

Near 40 million people live in 23 primarily Republican States across the US and are represented in Congress by 46 senators. This equals the population of California, represented by only 2. What happens to democracy when the majority of citizens are not equitably represented?

Activate the will of the majority! |

BUILDING BLOCK

Naming the Drivers of Inequality

Confronting inequality begins by naming what produces it. We have identified 12 drivers of inequality, and created a program of action for each of them, as the foundation for design. The aim is to articulate a new value system, to reorganize and reform institutional priorities and modes of representation.

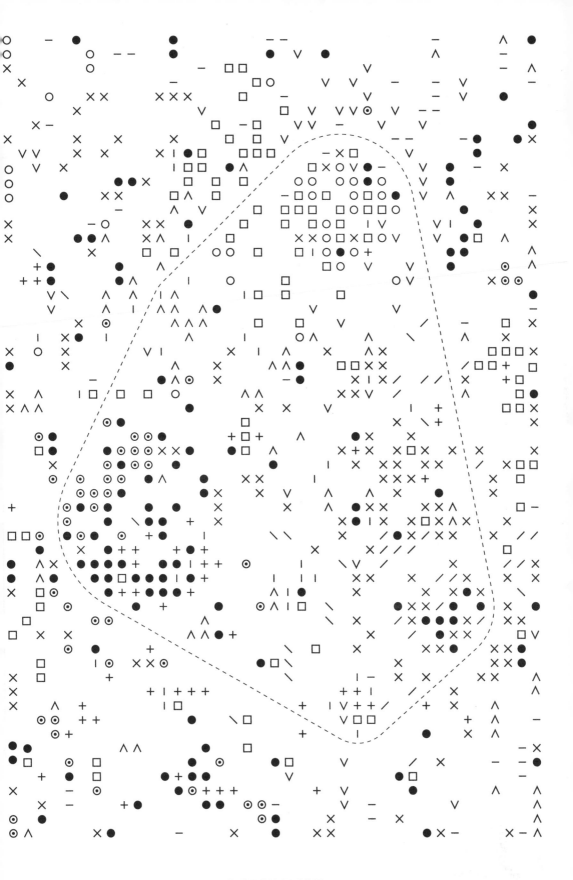

BUILDING BLOCKS

Construct the Political

Neutrality is Complicity

"There continues to be an inability to envisage the problems facing our societies today in a political way. Political questions always involve decisions, which require us to make a choice between conflicting alternatives."
Chantal Mouffe, *The Return of the Political*

To remain neutral in the face of today's social and economic injustices is to be complicit with norms, institutions and policies that perpetuate what is ethically and morally wrong. To think more socially and politically is to prioritize, to take a position:
That inequality is wrong
That xenophobia is wrong
That building border walls is wrong.

Periods when private interests dominate often coincide with a collective refusal to think politically. Too often our creative design fields align uncritically with neoliberal agendas, spatializing, unifying and materializing a consensus politics of free-market economics into an apolitical formalist project of beautification that camouflages disparity, and whose relentless homogeneity hides any vestige of difference.

02

Return Duchamp's Urinal to the Bathroom!

In a conversation with performance artist Tania Bruguera about rethinking artistic practices in an era of unprecedented inequality, she suggested that we return Duchamp's urinal to the bathroom! Perpetuating the notion of a *free imagination* as a creative prophylactic keeps us at a safe and neutral distance from crisis. What we need instead is an *urgent imagination* to engage in institutional critique, anticipating modes of action to alter stagnant and exclusionary political and economic structures, and to advocate for a more committed relationship between art and the everyday, closing the gap between social responsibility, political engagement and artistic experimentation. We advocate not for political architecture but for reconstructing the political itself.

A Map of Detours

Urban and social justice demand taking a position against neoliberal urban growth and its institutions. Equitable urban policy demands altering the conventional meanings of infrastructure, density, zoning, and sustainability.

Affordable housing demands real changes in housing policy and economy. These are political projects: we are not only designers of things but also of political, economic and civic processes.

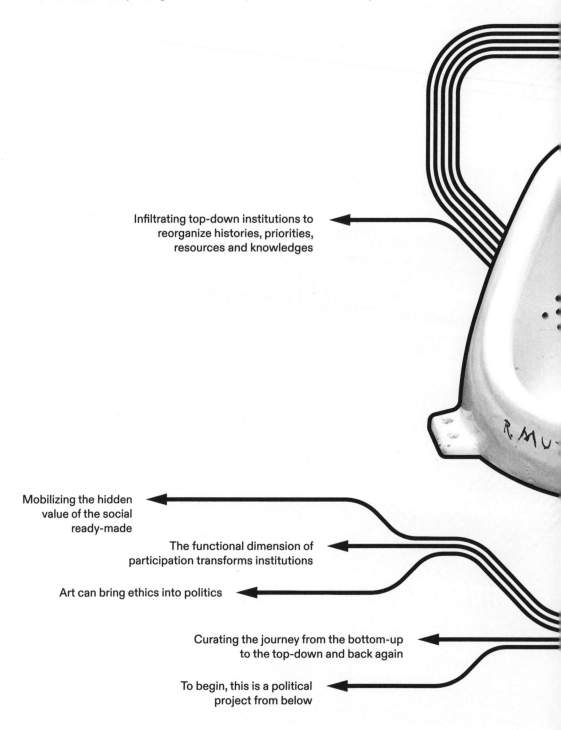

Infiltrating top-down institutions to reorganize histories, priorities, resources and knowledges

Mobilizing the hidden value of the social ready-made

The functional dimension of participation transforms institutions

Art can bring ethics into politics

Curating the journey from the bottom-up to the top-down and back again

To begin, this is a political project from below

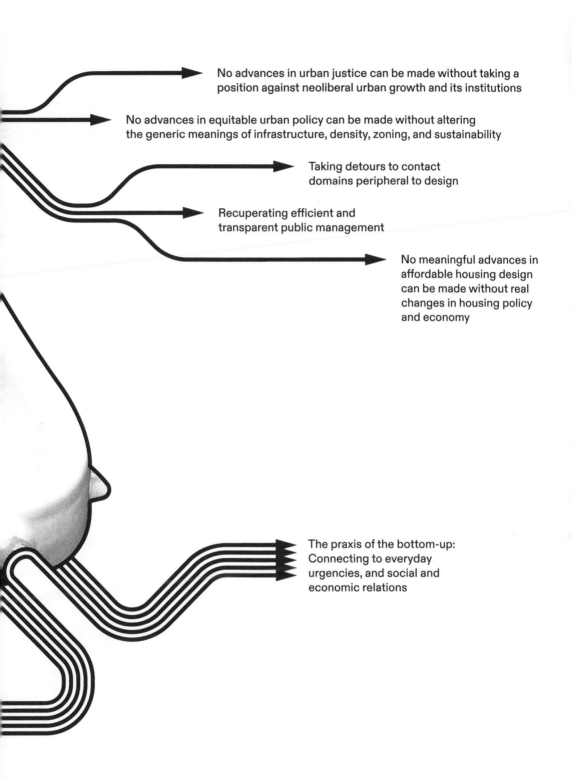

No advances in urban justice can be made without taking a position against neoliberal urban growth and its institutions

No advances in equitable urban policy can be made without altering the generic meanings of infrastructure, density, zoning, and sustainability

Taking detours to contact domains peripheral to design

Recuperating efficient and transparent public management

No meaningful advances in affordable housing design can be made without real changes in housing policy and economy

The praxis of the bottom-up: Connecting to everyday urgencies, and social and economic relations

Recuperate Institutional Memory

Where is the New Deal?

As we confront ideologies of austerity, history demonstrates that public investment need not be understood as a drain on the economy, but as a stimulant that produces more equitable economic growth. When accompanied by inclusive and accountable governance, and a robust social safety net, it is also a tool for social equity. Broadly speaking, after the economic crash of 1929 until the late 1970s, the New Deal prioritized public thinking, transformed governance, and reformed institutions to advance a redistributive economic agenda designed to mitigate poverty and maximize opportunity. Most casual references to the New Deal focus on FDR himself, on legislative agendas or the infrastructural achievements themselves. But we believe the American public can learn more today from the political and civic processes that enabled these projects to happen. It is important to reassemble forensically how a collective desire for change instigated action, seeking clues and operational traces to mine the complexity of political and civic process that generated so many iconic urban and institutional transformations and interventions. It is equally important today to refresh and adapt these critical histories to new urgencies, with new tools for implementation, new actors and new processes, to produce even more effective responses to social injustice, inequality, infrastructural defunding, and the erosion of the social safety net. Can designers be the interlocutors of institutional memory?

03

American ~~Dream~~ Nightmare?

n their powerful study of American inequality political economists Emmanuel Saez and Thomas Piketty documented a public-private pendulum that swung back and forth during the 20th century between periods of public investment and austerity.[3] Their research revealed that during the last 100 years, the two greatest moments of economic crisis and income inequality—the Great Depression of 1929 and the 2008 recession—were also periods of the lowest marginal taxation of wealth. At bottom, they exposed the trickle-down hypocrisy of the American Dream—that we all benefit when we forgive the wealthy their taxes.

Income inequality in the United States, 1910–2010

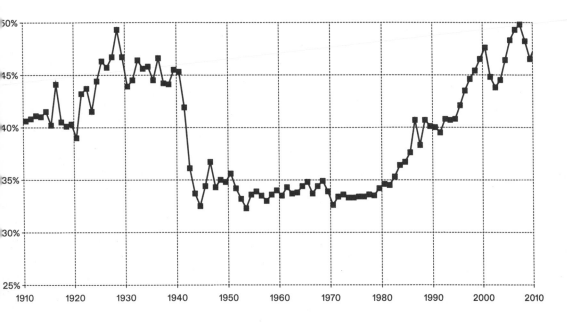

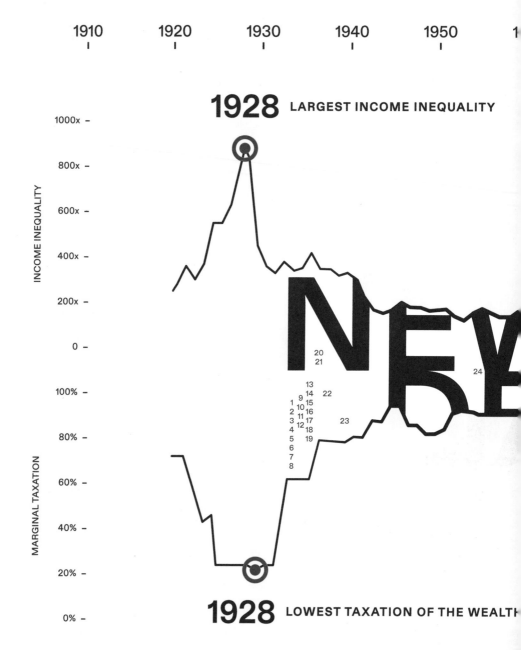

1928 LARGEST INCOME INEQUALITY

1000x –

800x –

600x –

400x –

200x –

0 –

INCOME INEQUALITY

20
21

13
14   22
9   15
1   10   16
2   11   17   23
3   12   18
4   19
5
6
7
8

24

100% –

80% –

60% –

40% –

20% –

0% –

MARGINAL TAXATION

1928 LOWEST TAXATION OF THE WEALTH

BUILDING BLOCK

Saez-Piketty Redux

Two lines bend across time and mirror each other. Two peaks at the ends and a valley in the middle. The two peaks represent moments of dramatic income inequality in America. Piketty and Saez demonstrate that at these two critical points the richest 1% owned more wealth than the bottom 90%, a gap that would narrow dramatically during the decades of the New Deal, when a public-minded political leadership mobilized cross-sector civic commitments to tackle inequality, supported by progressive taxation, and the redistribution of wealth to benefit public investment in infrastructure and the social safety net. While racism and segregation still organized urban life in America, the New Deal advanced housing, immigration, labor and civil rights. Can we recuperate civic lineages to support structural political and cultural transformation today, in an era of deepening inequality?

1980 1990 2000 2010 2020

LARGEST INCOME INEQUALITY **2008**

LOWEST TAXATION OF THE WEALTHY **2008**

61 62 63
52 60
53
54 55 56
57 64
58 65
59 66
67 70
68
69

· Agricultural Adjustment Act · 2 · Civil Works Administration · 3 · Civilian Conservation Corps · 4 · Federal Parks Reorganization Act · 5 · Federal Surplus Commodities Corporation · 6 · Glass-Steagall Act · 7 · Home Owners Loan Corporation · 8 · National Industrial Recovery Act · 9 · Communications Act · 10 · Federal Housing Administration · 11 · Fish and Wildlife Conservation Acts · 12 · National Housing Act · 13 · Federal Arts Projects Act · 14 · National Labor Relations Act · 15 · National Youth Administration Act · 16 · Public Utility holding Company Act · 17 · Relief Art Projects Act · 18 · Social Security Act · 19 · Works Progress Administration · 20 · Rural Electrification Act · 21 · Soil Conservation Act · 22 · Farm Security Administration · 23 · Federal Security Agency · 24 · Housing Act · 25 · Migration and Refugee Assistance Act · 26 · Peace Corps Act · 27 · Economic Opportunity Act · 28 · Equal Pay Act · 29 · Civil Rights Act · 30 · Food Stamp Act · 31 · Land and Water Conservation Act · 32 · Child Nutrition Act · 33 · Elementary and Second Education Act · 34 · Freedom of Information Act · 35 · Food and Agriculture Act · 36 · Higher Education Act 37 · Housing and Urban Development Act · 38 · National Historic Preservation Act · 39 · National Foundation on the Arts and the Humanities Act · 40 · Older Americans Act · 41 · Public Works and Economic Development Act · 42 · Voting Rights Act · 43 · Demonstration Cities and Metropolitan Development Act · 44 · National and Wildlife Refuge System Administration Act · 45 · Public Broadcasting Act · 46 · Gun Control Act · 47 · National Parks Foundation Act · 48 · National Trail System Act · 49 · Clean Air Act · 50 · Clean Water Act · 51 · National Environmental Protection Act · 52 · National Cancer Act · 53 · Federal Aid Highway Act · 54 · Endangered Species Act · 55 · Disaster Relief Act · 56 · Family Educational Rights and Privacy Act · 57 · Indian Self-Determination and Assistance Act · 58 · National Health Planning and Resources Development Act · 59 · Research on Aging Act · 60 · Education for All Handicapped Children Act · 61 · National Forest Management Act · 62 · Community Reinvestment Act · 63 · Department of Energy Organization Act · 64 · Civil Service Reform Act · 65 · Ethics in Government Act · 66 · Indian Child Welfare Act · 67 · Energy Tax Act · 68 · National Energy Conservation Policy Act · 69 · Nuclear Non-Proliferation Act · 70 · Department of Education Organization Act

BUILDING BLOCKS

Decolonize Knowledge

Visualizing Urban Histories of Racial Injustice

We must recontextualize history to expose the roots and springs of racism and social injustice, to piece together the conditions and knowledges that have naturalized the "macro-aggressions" of history, and official accounts of who "we" are, who "they" are. We must fill in the voids hollowed out by design across the histories of oppression, reconstructing facts that have been erased, silenced, disciplined by institutions of power. Daylighting repressed social memory requires decolonizing knowledges. We see visualization as a powerful tool in this cultural project. The histories and structures of systemic racism and their spatial manifestations in the city must be visualized in order to agitate entrenched norms and begin the collective process of reconstructing a new social and political ground. No architectural and urban intervention in the city should begin without asking: Whose land was this? Where are we building? Why? Every project must acknowledge by visualizing the contested histories inscribed in space, the lineages of racism and marginalization, displacement and disinvestment, ownership and belonging to expose the neoliberal fallacy of *terra nullius* and speculative urban territories of amnesia.

04

Cumulative Impacts of Racism, Redlining, Disinvestment and Climate Change

Our work is committed to the most marginalized sectors of the city. Every project begins with a critical diagram that visualizes the historical, spatial and ecological vectors that situate a zone of engagement. These early queries yield an operative field of conflicts and their compounding impacts on the lives of inhabitants as the basis of our design process. An example is our adaptation of a redlining map of Southeast San Diego from 1932. These maps were ubiquitous across US cities, weapons of urban warfare used by financial institutions to deny access and services to primarily Black and Latinx communities, preventing social and economic development. Here we have overlayed and historicized the map with current socioeconomic and environmental data to visualize the cumulative impacts of racism, exclusion, disinvestment, gerrymandering and climate change on these deliberately marginalized neighborhoods. Little surprise this area remains the largest Black community in the region, characterized by high unemployment, low educational attainment, food insecurity and cyclical poverty. Little surprise that it has the least urban tree canopy, the greatest heat island effects and the most contaminated waterways in the region. We also discovered that this zone lies at the heart of a sacred Indigenous environment, a historic Kumeyaay watershed that has been fractured by centuries of urban development.

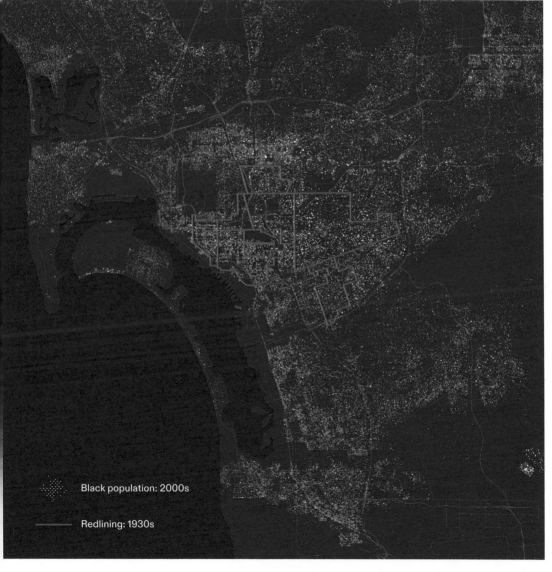

Black population: 2000s

Redlining: 1930s

Epistemic Justice in Design: Co-producing Knowledge

Social justice demands not only a redistribution of resources but also a redistribution of knowledges. Shifting power relations means committing to restorative practices that hold top-down policies and allocations accountable to bottom-up knowledges and priorities. We must reposition histories of injustice to structure new approaches to policy-making and public investment in marginalized communities and neglected bio-regions. *Epistemic Justice in Design* demands that we continually interrogate our assumptions, approaches and methods as architects and urban designers, that we carry an "empirical lantern" when we engage the world, as development economist Albert Hirschman called it, remaining open to learning from diverse epistemologies and practices, and that we strive to co-produce new knowledge with others as we design strategies to tackle injustice. Only by *translating* and *redistributing* diverse knowledges and practices can we decolonize urban and environmental thinking, mobilize fresh ideas and languages about equity, sustainability and resilience, transform urban policy and spatialize justice in our cities and hinterlands.

The Kumeyaay Rock Drop: Intersectional Literacies

Michael Connolly-Miskwish, an elder of the Kumeyaay Nation and a frequent collaborator of ours, proposed that we could learn a lot about climate adaptation from his tribe's approaches to water management. He explained that water was the spatial organizing system for Kumeyaay clans (Sh'mulq), who used watershed boundaries to define their territories and situate communal life. Oral histories narrate the traditional practice of "rock drop" to confront drought conditions. Piling rocks and brush in drainage zones helps to recharge streams, raise water tables and fortify the boundaries of the wetlands. Wetland restoration is also the key to maintaining supplies of food, medicine and building materials, including reinvigorating the juncus, a root used in basket weaving, a source of local economy.

1. Translating Knowledges	2. Redistributing Knowledges
Confronting climate change requires top-down planetary coordination of policy, finance and clean energy technologies deployed equitably at grand scales to replace our dependence on fossil fuels. It also demands that we cultivate a new value system from the bottom-up, along with new ways of thinking and doing. Learning from Kumeyaay practices has transformed our design practice, and illustrates a kind of paradigm shift that we believe can decolonize power relations, integrate what our technocratic and bureaucratic ways of thinking and doing have divided, and inspire new approaches to community and economic development. Our engagement with Kumeyaay elders taught us that oral history is generative; that water is social; that science is embedded in the everyday; that civic participation can yield bottom-up technologies for habitat restoration, cultural sustainability and economy; and that recognition of bottom-up strategies can help to stimulate a new urban-ecological public imagination.	Spatializing justice requires new platforms for horizontal dialogue and mutual learning between communities and institutions—two-way flows that bring the knowledges and practices of communities into public reflection and decision-making and academic research, and bring the resources, knowledges and tools of public institutions and universities to communities in order to fortify bottom-up agency and capacity for political and climate action. Architects and designers can create these new spaces and platforms for encounter, dialogue, pedagogy, collaboration and political representation. We can also partner with communities to co-design and participate in the exchanges themselves, and develop tools that visualize invisible histories and experiences of oppression, to mobilize broader cultural recognition and reflection and institutional accountability. Ultimately, we can help facilitate the movement of knowledges and resources from the bottom-up to the top-down, and back again.

Indigenous traditional knowledges

Oral history as praxis

Science is embedded in the everyday life of communities

Integrative community-led practices for habitat, fire and water management

Rock Drop infrastructures for wetland restoration

Juncus root harvesting for basket weaving

Linking social, environmental, cultural and economic productivity

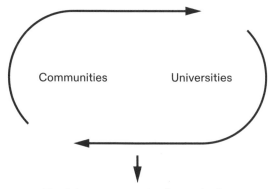

Communities   Universities

Fresh languages and epistemologies

BUILDING BLOCKS

Radicalize the Local

From Ambiguity to Specificity

Geopolitics is always an intensely local experience. We need to move beyond the abstraction of the "global" to engage local zones of conflict, where injustice hits the ground. Localizing the global does not mean retreating to protectionism, or the myopic agendas of identitarian politics. For us, radicalizing the local means repositioning ourselves in local dynamics to expose the drivers and institutional histories of injustice, discriminatory public policies and unscrupulous political actors in a particular place.

It means investigating how global dynamics manifest in local contexts. In this sense, our work moves from a *critical distance* (engagement with an "out there" somewhere) to a *critical proximity* (engagement with the "here and now" of the local territory and its immediate social-political context). By radicalizing the local, we socialize and politicize the universal in local spaces of accountability, where our theoretical assumptions can be grounded through praxis and through solidaristic modes of activism.

05

A Critical Proximity

Proximity is not only a geographical or spatial concept but also an institutional one. In the 1970s Peter Bürger drew upon the foundational principles of the *avant-garde* to advocate taking a "critical distance" from the corporate colonization of art—a stance from the outside.[4] While gaining a less embedded vantage obviously has merit, we believe that today's urgencies demand a "critical proximity"—new strategies of infiltration into institutions and cultures of injustice. We need to penetrate into local political hegemonies and identify ways to alter discriminatory urban policy. We cannot step aside and surrender public institutions to the forces and flows of capitalism and nationalism. We see radical potential in bottom-up urban and regulatory alterations that trickle up to transform top-down institutions and policies.

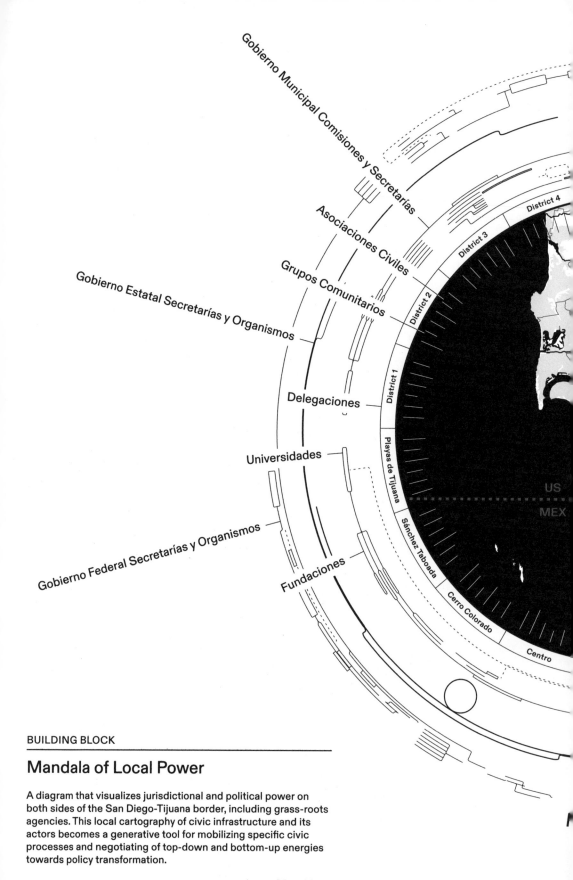

Gobierno Municipal Comisiones y Secretarías

Asociaciones Civiles

Grupos Comunitarios

Gobierno Estatal Secretarías y Organismos

Delegaciones

Universidades

Gobierno Federal Secretarías y Organismos

Fundaciones

District 4

District 3

District 2

District 1

Playas de Tijuana

Sánchez Taboada

Cerro Colorado

Centro

US
MEX

BUILDING BLOCK

Mandala of Local Power

A diagram that visualizes jurisdictional and political power on
both sides of the San Diego-Tijuana border, including grass-roots
agencies. This local cartography of civic infrastructure and its
actors becomes a generative tool for mobilizing specific civic
processes and negotiating of top-down and bottom-up energies
towards policy transformation.

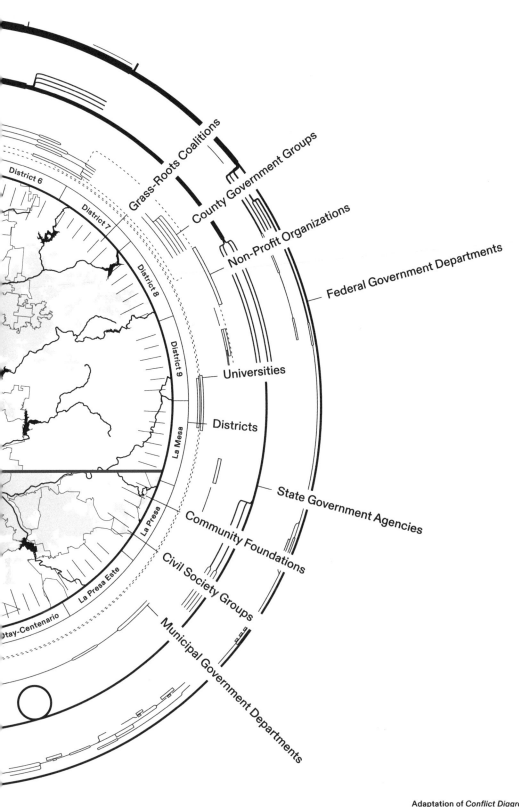

District 6
District 7
District 8
District 9
La Mesa
La Presa
La Presa Este
Otay-Centenario

Grass-Roots Coalitions
County Government Groups
Non-Profit Organizations
Federal Government Departments
Universities
Districts
State Government Agencies
Community Foundations
Civil Society Groups
Municipal Government Departments

Adaptation of *Conflict Diagram* by
Page Comeaux and Rachel Lefevre,
Advanced Design Studio,
Yale School of Architecture, 2019.

BUILDING BLOCKS

Visualize Urban Conflict

Urban Conflict is Our Creative Tool

Critical intervention into the urban field requires recognizing the contested spatial and institutional power dynamics that drive today's urban crises. Exposing this often-missing information enables us to piece together a more accurate, anticipatory urban research and design intervention. In other words, the conditions themselves, the institutional mechanisms that produced the crisis, are our materials for design, making urban conflict an important creative tool to reimagine the city today—a generative platform from which to develop policy proposals and urban development strategies. The complexity of the metropolitan condition should solicit more experimental architectures, committed to exposing, visualizing and engaging urban conflict as the radical context from which to problematize the relationship between the social, the political, and the aesthetic.

06

Architectures of Dissensus

Political philosopher Chantal Mouffe characterizes the crisis of contemporary democracy as an inability to envisage social problems in a political way.[5] For many, democracy is equated with the resolution of conflict, a process to bring about a harmonious end of contestation freeing people from public concerns to engage in private consumption. For Mouffe, democracy is inherently agonistic, a process through which deep social conflicts emerge into public light, become visible to the powerless, and ultimately force societies to make hard choices among irreconcilable alternatives. Through this lens, architectural and urban projects and initiatives oriented towards social justice must begin by recognizing the conflicts and controversies that situate the object of study, and engage the institutions responsible for them, as well as the communities most affected by them. For us, tackling emergency housing in Tijuana's informal settlements, for example, begins with visualizing the conflicts between multinational factories, the politics of cheap labor and informal urbanization.

- Conflict between forces of urbanization and topographic landscape
- Conflict between jurisdictional and hydrological boundaries
- Conflict between political and natural systems
- Conflict between freeways, watersheds and neighborhoods
- Conflict between private and public property
- Conflict between urban and ecological flows
- Conflict between enclaves of wealth and poverty
- Conflict between land-use and social life
- Conflict between sprawl and regional environmental resources
- Conflict between vertical and horizontal urban growth
- Conflict between top-down and bottom-up urbanization

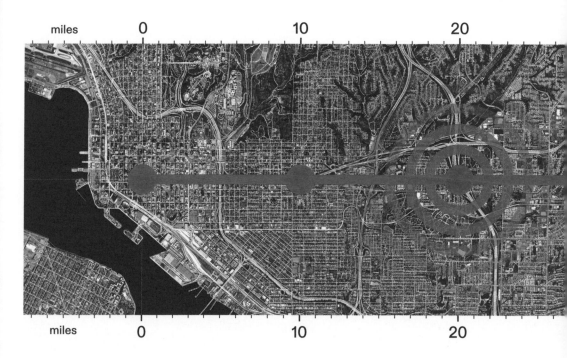

San Diego, 2021. Google Earth.

60 Linear Miles of Urban Conflict

Imagine a 60 linear-mile cross-section of any city in the world, beginning in the city center and moving southeast, ending in the city's periphery. This urban-territorial "cut" will inevitably compress the most dramatic issues challenging our conventional ideas of architecture and urbanism. We will find along this trajectory a set of collisions, critical junctures, and conflicts between natural and artificial ecologies, between top-down forces of urbanization and bottom-up social and ecological networks. Contemporary artistic practice needs to reposition itself within sites of urban and territorial conflict to expose their often-shrouded institutional histories. Visualizing conflict means retroactively tracing and projectively modifying the backward discriminatory policies that have produced these collisions.

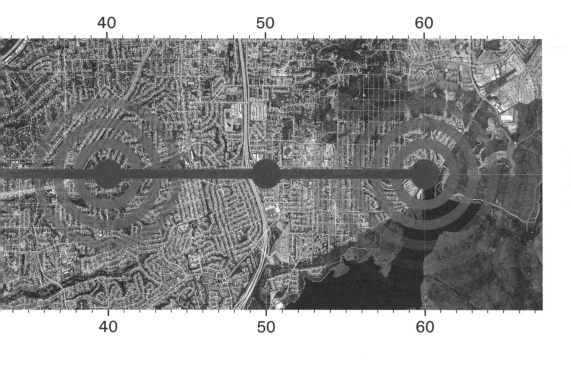

Transgress Borders

The Wall Exists Only to be Transgressed

We are witnessing the militarization of borders everywhere, aligned with legislation that erodes public institutions and norms, barricades public space and ultimately divides communities. These protectionist strategies are fueled by nationalist paranoia and greed that threaten to dominate public life for years to come. While nationalist political narratives always characterize borders as sites of division and control, everyday life in this part of the world is shaped by regular flows and circulations across the wall. Tijuana artist Marcos Ramirez ERRE once told us that border walls exist only to be transgressed—and isn't that the ultimate aspiration of art? To transgress our own conventions and fears? When a community's productive capacity is disrupted by jurisdictional power, it is necessary to find a means of recuperating its agency. This is a ripe space of intervention for art and architecture practice today.

07

Chronology of an Invasion

Mobilized by the lack of skateboard parks in the city, a group of young skateboarders invaded a vacant space below a San Diego freeway off-ramp to build their own skateboard park. We recorded the process. It is not enough to protest an issue, they suggested; it is important that there is also a strategy, a process, to engage and transgress the issue, even if it means encroaching illegally beyond jurisdictional borders to reclaim unused public space. Armed with shovels, they invaded the underpass, and their urban performance became the catalyst for a political process to negotiate jurisdictional power in the midst of the collision between large freeway infrastructure and their neighborhood. Two weeks after they encroached into the abandoned space to reshape the ground, they were stopped by the police and evicted from the underpass. They decided to challenge

the municipality and its legislation over public space. Having transgressed this invisible urban border, the young skaters asked questions that designers seldom ask: *Who owns this territory, and who owns the resources? Who are the institutions represented here? What is the municipal definition of public space? Why does public space legislation not include our activity? How do we construct a process to access and manage this unused space?* They won their case. Their NGO, the Washington Skate Board Park, was given a lease to the site for 1¢/year, framed by an agreement to manage and sustain the space, with economic support and programmatic activity. This bottom-up act of transgression by a group of young skaters opened a political process that transformed top-down urban policy.

Adaptation of *The Naked City*,
Guy Debord, 1957.

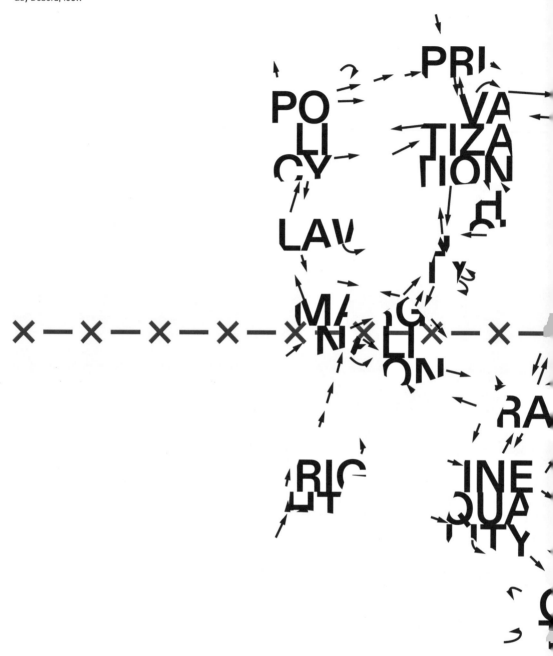

Deborder: Urbanizations Beyond the Property Line

Guy Debord's *Naked City* diagram is a building block for all urban border crossers. It does not belong to Paris but to metropolitan zones everywhere, where borders emerge from the collision of the top-down and the bottom-up. As the Situationists imagined it, the decisive *avant-garde* moment occurs when an ordinary citizen becomes insurgent and encroaches into the gaps, ruptures, unfinished and leftover urban spaces to pursue opportunities seemingly foreclosed by the rigidity of the formal city.

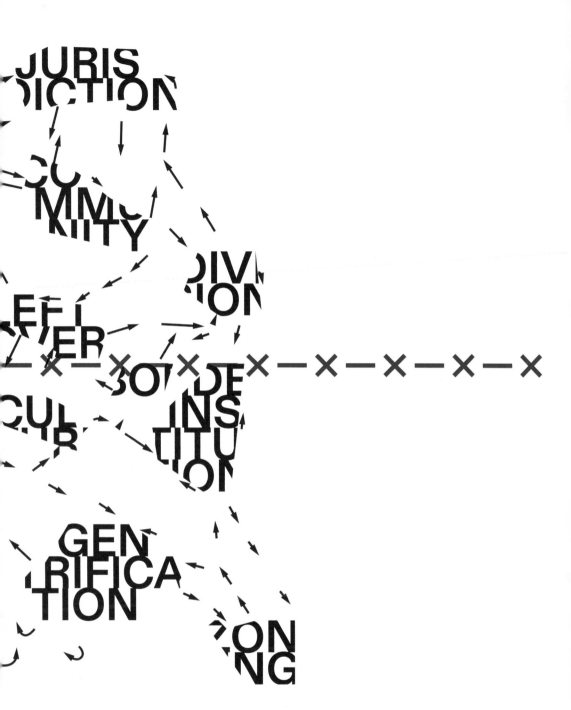

JURIS
DICTION

COMM
UNITY

DIVI
SION

REFLE
CTER

BOR
DE

CUR
B

INS
TITU
TION

GEN
TRIFICA
TION

ZON
ING

Reimagine Jurisdiction

The Conflict Between the Natural and the Political

Confronting climate change and building more just and resilient cities requires radical transformation of conventional approaches to urbanization that prioritize the administrative over the natural. Cities are a mosaic of property lines, imposed onto complex topographic boundaries. The bulldozers of enclosure and exclusion ignore how ecologies perform, and undermine the social and environmental resilience in our cities. Put another way, urbanization unfolds through a lopsided contest between the administrative and the natural, stewarded by the denizens of urban development who seek to flatten the messiness of ecological systems to build their dream-castles. Profits turn the urban and the ecological into enemies, embroiled in a war where the ultimate losers are our collective environmental assets and our productive landscapes. Ironically, the *tabula rasae* that proliferate through the city always memorialize the erasures, the ecologies they destroy, with such tragic names as "Riverwalk," "Golden Creek" or "Linda Vista."

08

Dumb Sovereignty: Nation Against Nature

Only the most myopic or racist of nationalist politics can conclude that walling the other will solve our problems. While the border wall satisfies protectionist urges for physical security, it ultimately produces environmental insecurity, harming the ecologies essential to the health and sustainability of the region. In our research-based practice, we seek to expose the self-destructive spatial impulses of nationalism—deconstructing the national through the natural—by visualizing the ecological systems that walls cannot contain: hydrologic basins, indigenous lands, ecological and wildlife corridors and migratory flows. Over the years we have archived aerial images of precise moments along the continental border between the US and Mexico where the jurisdictional line of the nation collides with natural systems—where the wall becomes a knife inflicting environmental wounds on the territory, harming both sides. Instead of an arbitrary 19th-century line imposed onto complex systems, the border should yield to ecological realities and thicken into a shared bioregion.

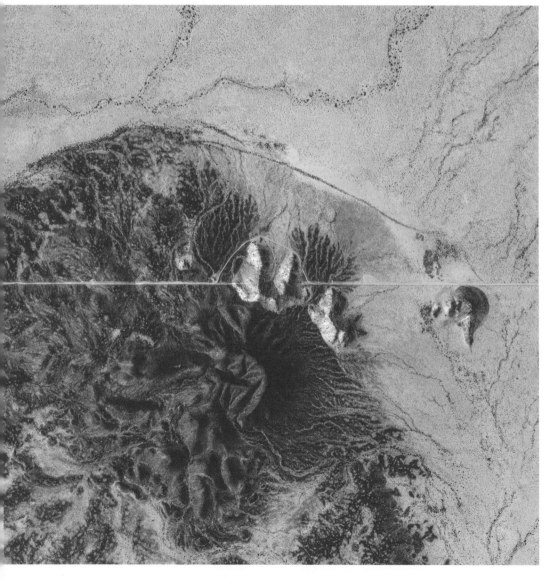

BUILDING BLOCKS

Micro-Basins as Neighborhoods

Binational regions across the world are uniquely positioned to reimagine borders and belonging through the logics of natural and social systems, and reconceptualize sovereignty through shared environmental assets and the imperatives of bioregional interdependence. These geopolitical conditions are reproduced at very local scales as well, as neighborhoods are regularly fragmented by arbitrary jurisdictional power, obscuring the recognition of natural and social boundaries as an organizing framework for collective agency. Instead of fragmenting the territory through jurisdictional lines, can hydrological boundaries construct community? Can specific micro-basins within a watershed system demarcate and construct a neighborhood? We are calling for a post-jurisdictional imagination, where natural and social boundaries, not political ones, organize the city, and the relations between the urban, the social and the ecological.

Administrative boundaries

Hydrological boundaries

Creeks

BUILDING BLOCKS

Complicate Autonomy

Challenging Self-Referentiality

Autonomy in architecture evokes a pervasive indifference to the socio-economic and political material that complicates architectural form. It is a recurring utopian dream that form can bring order to the chaos of social difference, that structural and compositional strategies can bring political, cultural and aesthetic unity to a society run amok. While we agree with a recent political stance in architecture that a return to autonomy can fortify resistance against the aesthetic relativism of speculative hyper-capitalism, we are critical of a nostalgic return to top-down autonomous and self-referential language as the only way out of this ongoing post-modern nightmare. While we also agree with critiques of autonomy oriented towards the bottom-up consumerist politics of capitalism, we equally condemn the abandonment of bottom-up social movements and the contested spaces between the public and the private. After all, in the absence of a progressive welfare state that can reinstate a public and social agenda at a massive scale, who will build these architectural dream-castles today if not anti-democratic governments, autocratic dictatorships and corporate power?

09

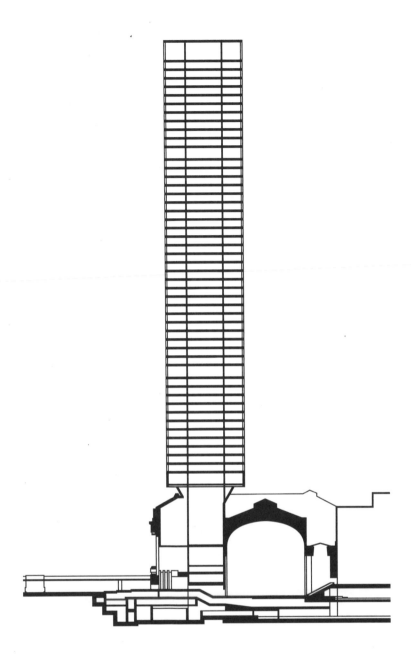

Autonomy and the Metropolitan Battlefield

The algorithms of formal parametric composition suffer from a *precariousness of omission*, as the set of parameters that are selected for the assembly of self-organizing patterns, volumes and effects (which can, in any given context, be the same, from a doorknob to an entire city!) respond to an astonishingly reductive set of formal attributes that always exclude the complex dynamics of the metropolitan battlefield. Anticipating the triviality of these autonomous formal games in years to come,

Rem Koolhaas observed in the 1990s that the former Pan Am building above Grand Central Station, despite its "clumsiness" and bad details, was the most revolutionary building in New York City, as it had intervened in the contested space of air-rights, floating above the historical landmark by exploiting the politics of verticality, not through *a priori* formalist, autonomous and self-referential exterior form, but through sectional complexity and programmatic flows.[6]

Relational Architectures

The problems of the contemporary city are systemic problems that need deeper ecological thinking. Fritjof Capra's notion of "deep ecology" illustrates this very well, suggesting the need to challenge conventional meanings of ecology.[7] The ecology of a bicycle, for example, pertains to the functional relationship of the parts of the bicycle to each other. A deeper ecology of this bicycle would ask instead: Who produces this bicycle? Where? With what materials, sourced from where? And what is its cultural application? The cultural consciousness of bike-riding varies in California, India and Denmark. A new, more experimental political economy of architectural form can be found today in the construction of new social-economic and political "envelopes" that incorporate the political, social and economic domains that have been absent from self-organizing formal logics of architecture.

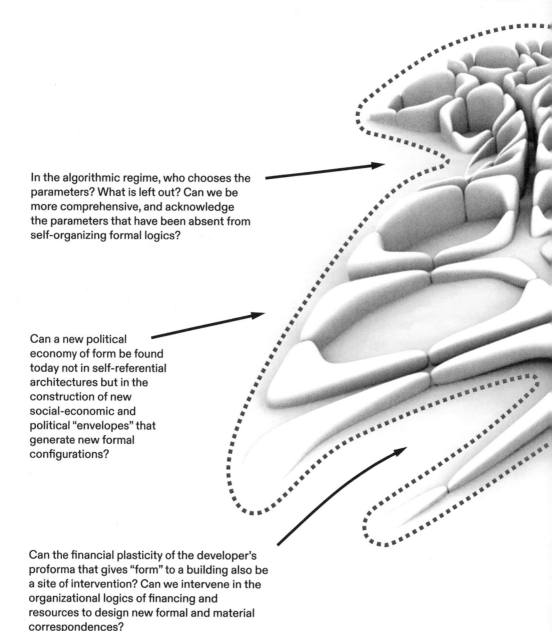

In the algorithmic regime, who chooses the parameters? What is left out? Can we be more comprehensive, and acknowledge the parameters that have been absent from self-organizing formal logics?

Can a new political economy of form be found today not in self-referential architectures but in the construction of new social-economic and political "envelopes" that generate new formal configurations?

Can the financial plasticity of the developer's proforma that gives "form" to a building also be a site of intervention? Can we intervene in the organizational logics of financing and resources to design new formal and material correspondences?

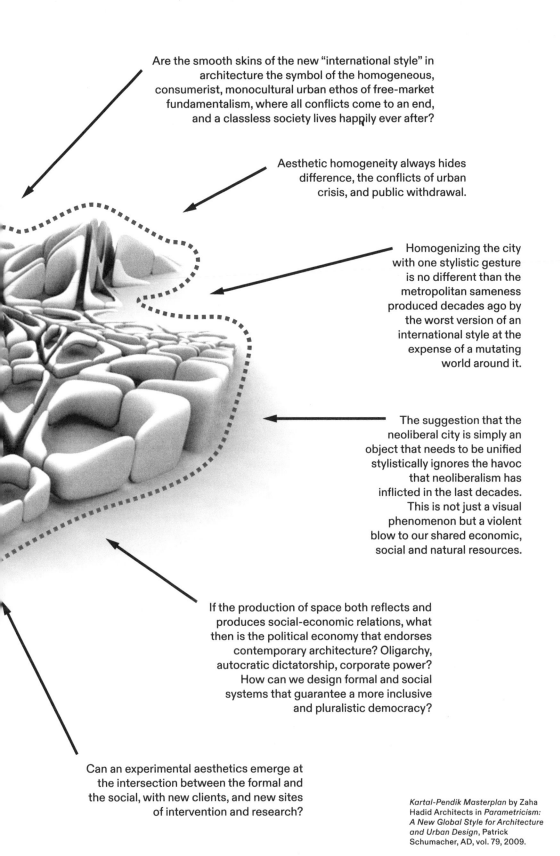

Are the smooth skins of the new "international style" in architecture the symbol of the homogeneous, consumerist, monocultural urban ethos of free-market fundamentalism, where all conflicts come to an end, and a classless society lives happily ever after?

Aesthetic homogeneity always hides difference, the conflicts of urban crisis, and public withdrawal.

Homogenizing the city with one stylistic gesture is no different than the metropolitan sameness produced decades ago by the worst version of an international style at the expense of a mutating world around it.

The suggestion that the neoliberal city is simply an object that needs to be unified stylistically ignores the havoc that neoliberalism has inflicted in the last decades. This is not just a visual phenomenon but a violent blow to our shared economic, social and natural resources.

If the production of space both reflects and produces social-economic relations, what then is the political economy that endorses contemporary architecture? Oligarchy, autocratic dictatorship, corporate power? How can we design formal and social systems that guarantee a more inclusive and pluralistic democracy?

Can an experimental aesthetics emerge at the intersection between the formal and the social, with new clients, and new sites of intervention and research?

Kartal-Pendik Masterplan by Zaha Hadid Architects in *Parametricism: A New Global Style for Architecture and Urban Design*, Patrick Schumacher, AD, vol. 79, 2009.

BUILDING BLOCKS

Temporalize Infrastructure

Infrastructure is a Verb

There is no such thing as a natural disaster. As landscape architect Anuradha Mathur reminds us, disasters happen when nature collides with stupid urbanization, when we build where we shouldn't, when we think one-dimensionally about infrastructure. While top-down infrastructure is often an instrument of colonization, fragmentation and division of ecologies, territories, neighborhoods, we must also decolonize the idea of infrastructure itself. Conventionally, infrastructure, like architecture, is thought of as an object, a thing. But while architecture is noun, infrastructure must be a verb. While architecture freezes and spatializes time, infrastructures activate and temporalize space. Infrastructures perform the interface between large and small, formal and informal, top down and bottom up, artificial and natural. Ultimately, infrastructures should modulate difference and democratize urbanization. By moving from the one to the many, infrastructures are mediating systems for social integration, a collective way of constructing the city. Instead of fixing the destiny of the city with closed-ended architectures, infrastructures open new horizons by socializing and ecologizing space, and anticipating urban transformation and inclusion. Social and environmental justice in the city depend on rethinking infrastructure as a mechanism to facilitate heterogeneity, plurality and multiplicity.

10

The Instant Market

Scenes 1–2
In Bangkok, a train traverses an informal settlement.

Scenes 3–4
The train moves in close proximity to people around it. After the last car passes, informal vending stalls immediately reclaim their space on the train tracks.

Scene 5–6
Within seconds an informal market is fully operational, reconstituting itself with movable furniture and expandable canopies.

In this story, we do not wish to romanticize risk, but rather to learn from the social intelligence that charges a space with capacity to transform from one thing to another in such a short time. This agility and flexibility should inspire our idea of infrastructure, facilitating spatial resilience and porosity to absorb the effects of climate change or the irruptions of human activity. Can public infrastructure change through time to accommodate different uses, different modes of encounter and points of access? The democratization of public space entails blurring boundaries and transforming the monouse and one-dimensionality of top-down infrastructure to accommodate emergent social algorithms and the performance of the bottom-up.

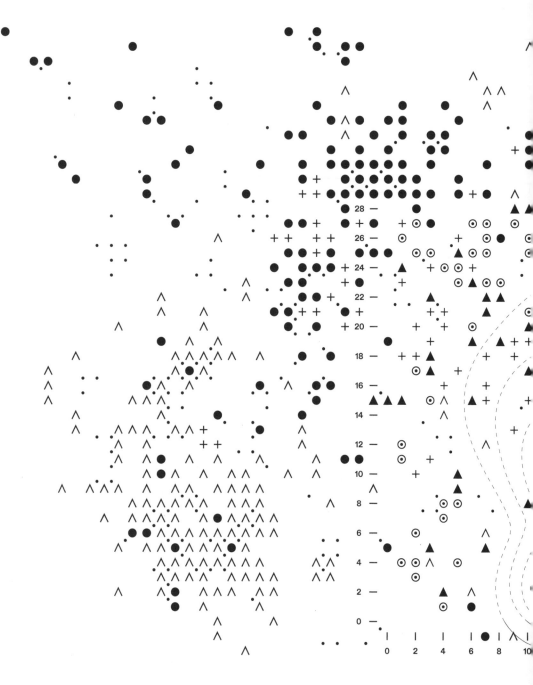

Socializing Infrastructural Urbanism

Stan Allen's essays *Infrastructural Urbanism* and *Field Conditions* are manifestos for our practice, to rethink the meaning of infrastructure through temporal and process-based dynamic systems, as well as more functional interfaces between top-down and bottom-up organizational logics to anticipate urban transformation.[8] We have adapted the main tenets of these theories in our work to conceptualize interdependences between physical, social and ecological systems, a point of departure to visualize the proportional relationship between infrastructural defunding and inequality, and the flexibility required to absorb difference and the informal spatial adaptations and social contingencies of migrant urbanization.

Translate the Informal

The Informal as Praxis

Instead of a fixed image or metaphor, we see the informal as a dynamic set of functional urban operations from below that counter and transgress the imposition of top-down jurisdictional power and exclusionary economic models. Ours is a practice of interpreting and translating the often-hidden procedures of informal urbanization into new strategies and tactics of urban intervention. We see the informal as the foundation for a new interpretation of urban justice, community and citizenship. For us, the informal is not just an aesthetic category; the informal is a praxis, mobilized by a socio-spatial intelligence detonated by urban survival.

11

Scaffolds for Things to Happen

Scene 1:
Tijuana's informal neighborhoods recycle the urban waste of San Diego.

Scene 2:
One day, a metal frame appears.

Scene 3:
A few weeks later, a recycled garage door is placed upon it.

Scene 4:
A couple months later, recycled wood begins to thread the spaces.

Scene 5:
Soon an informal house emerges.

The procedural intelligence of the informal detonates traditional notions of site-specificity and context into a more complex system of invisible social-economic exchanges. This operative dimension of the bottom-up needs translation to inspire new design strategies and new interventions in the formal city. We have always been interested in the emergent urban configurations produced in conditions of social emergency, and in the performative role of individuals and collectives in constructing their own spaces and self-governance practices. How can we as architects and designers engage the complex urban processes through which informal communities of practice manage time, boundaries, people, spaces, and resources simultaneously?

BUILDING BLOCKS

Anticipatory Urbanization	A
Elevating the socio-economic temporalities embedded in the informal to challenge the autonomy of buildings and their indifference to social inclusion.	

Temporalizing Materiality	B
Engaging the incremental material layering of informal urban dynamics, to question the *tabula rasa* approach of top-down planning.	

Representing Invisibility	C
When social organization happens first and spaces follow, the informal subverts established norms of urban representation, demanding a new socio-geographic political representation of the marginalized.	

Managing Complexity	D
Informal urbanization's simultaneous choreography of time, people, spaces and resources presents sophisticated management logics to support incrementality that are ungraspable by official planning agencies.	

Adaptive Growth	E
When generic spaces are adapted with informal micro-social and economic programmatic contingencies, the homogeneous largeness of official urbanization is transformed into more sustainable, plural and complex environments.	

Socializing Jurisdiction	F
Informal urbanization subordinates the arbitrariness of administrative boundaries by giving primacy to social and environmental boundaries as devices to construct community.	

Spatializing Capabilities	G
By absorbing the sweat equity of social participation, the incremental, low-cost layering of informal urban development redefines affordability, inspiring new paradigms of public infrastructure at the scale of neighborhoods.	

Ecologizing Density	H
The lightness and nomadism of the informal are procedures that inspire new conceptual interdependences between the urban and the ecological.	

Localizing the Political	I
Informal urbanization pixelates the political, producing new forms of local governance, along with the social guarantees that marginalized communities will control their own modes of productivity.	

Softening Property	J
The informal challenges existing models of property with a more inclusive idea of ownership, opening more porous and blurred designations between public and private.	

BUILDING BLOCK

Informal Algorithms

While it is compelling as architects to witness the material intelligence that emerges from urban crisis, we are aware of the dangers of fetishizing poverty. Engaging the informal in an ethical and epistemically just way demands a double project: 1) to expose the institutional mechanisms that have systematically and often through overtly racist and exclusionary policies produced the stigmas, and the political and economic forces that produce marginalization; and 2) to elevate the creative intelligence of marginalized communities, avoiding the trap of static victimization that has prevented the recognition of social and economic capabilities within informal urbanization, around which top-down support can be redirected. We believe there is much to learn from the emergent processes of informal development in settlements across the world, and that they can inspire a new political economy of urban growth for the contemporary city.

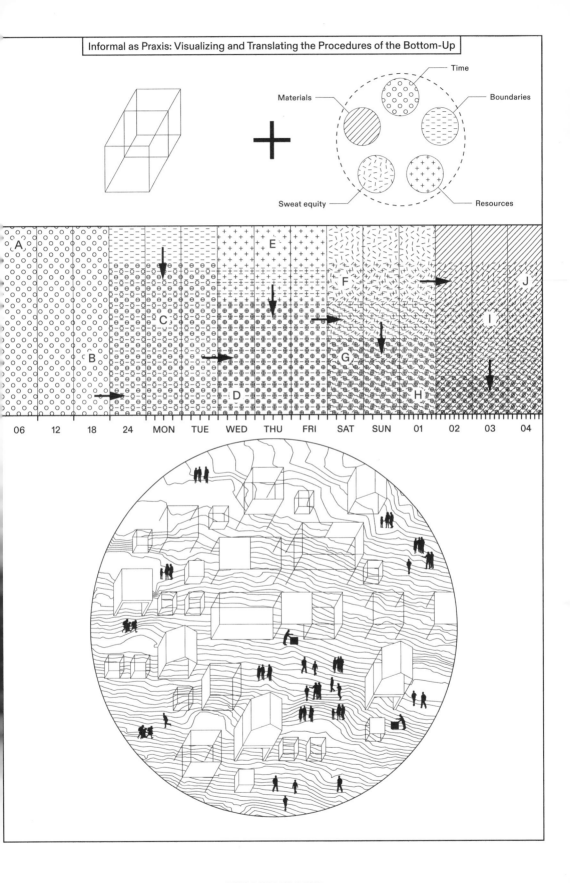

Informal as Praxis: Visualizing and Translating the Procedures of the Bottom-Up

Time
Materials
Boundaries
Sweat equity
Resources

06 12 18 24 MON TUE WED THU FRI SAT SUN 01 02 03 04

BUILDING BLOCKS

Perform Citizenship

Immigrant Civitas

Our recurring geopolitical crises at the San Diego-Tijuana border have provoked a more practical and fluid approach to citizenship, understood less as a formal identity validated by documents than as an experience of belonging that emerges through shared practices of living, surviving and resisting together in a disrupted civic and bioregional space. We have reconceptualized citizenship as a set of creative actions from below through which people in conditions of scarcity exercise solidaristic practices of coexistence and their collective right to the city. Immigrants carry these practical urban proclivities and capacities with them when they cross the border into San Diego. How can architecture spatialize and support the agency and entrepreneurial energies of these communities, where non-conforming economies and densities take physical form in the built environment as people accommodate the contingencies of everyday life?

12

Citizen-Architects

We have been inspired by stories of non-conforming spatial adaptations and retrofit by immigrants in San Diego's older inner-city neighborhoods. The *Nonconforming Buddha* is the story of a community of Buddhist monks who transformed a tiny postwar bungalow into a Buddhist temple. They acquired a small house in City Heights, a neighborhood in the southeast quadrant of the city. Although zoning permitted only a single-family residence there, the monks adapted the home into a temple, where they hosted meditations, as well as non-religious community events and services. As the functions of the temple grew, the monks informally retrofitted the original building, adding extra spaces, and then purchased the adjacent property, incrementally altering the small parcels into a social-economic infrastructure that provided support systems to the community.

Strategizing spatial adaptation

Sharing social ecologies

Solidaristic practices of survival

Empathy as political tool

Social organization as catalyst

Micro-politics for coexistence

Collaborative development

Mediating resources

Coordinating social cohesion

Reorganizing institutional protocols

Curating local economic productivity

Grounding rights to the city

Mapping "Nonconformity"

Urbanizations of retrofit are typically off the radar of conventional planning institutions. In our practice we visualize these bottom-up creative acts of resistance and citizenship, mapping anecdotes of adaptation by immigrants who, as citizen-architects, transform the spatial homogeneity of these neighborhoods into more complex social-economic environments. These become evidentiary tools for advocating transformations of top-down urban policy.

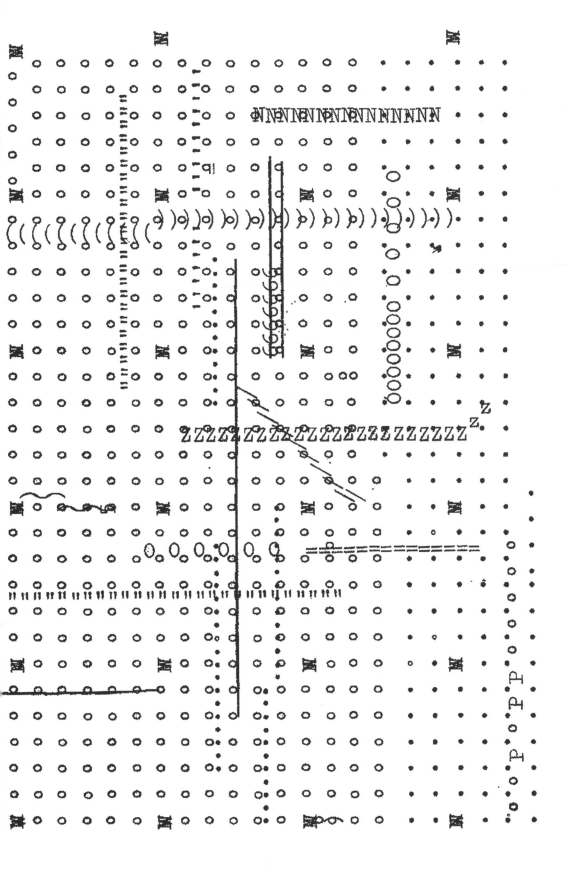

BUILDING BLOCKS

Socialize Density

Recalculating Density

Density should not be understood and measured as an abstract number of objects or people per area. This mentality produced irresponsible sprawl everywhere, where buildings are understood as "things" deposited indiscriminately across a territory without any relation to public infrastructure. Exclusionary urban growth is driven by this view of density, where buildings are commodities that fragment the city and undermine sociability. *Density must be understood instead as the intensity of social and economic exchanges per area.*

Migrant neighborhoods have taught us that the density of these exchanges mobilized by bottom-up urbanization is the DNA for democratizing the city, and for producing more inclusive and plural environments.

13

Challenging Selfish Sprawl:
McMansion Retrofitted

How do we anticipate density? We have documented the mutation of "bedroom-community" subdivisions in San Diego over the last decades from rigid, monocultural and one-dimensional zones into informal, multicultural and cross-programmed social ecologies. While this has been the trend across inner-city neighborhoods, in recent decades we have also witnessed a proliferation of McMansions everywhere, subsidized by an oil-hungry political economy of urban growth. Now that climate change is forcing us to confront ourselves and question our resource-depleting and consumerist ways of growing, will tactics of adaptation and retrofit determine the

future of this selfish sprawl? As we collect evidence of how the older subdivisions of the mid-city transformed radically through the contingencies of migrant urbanization, can we anticipate in the next five decades that the one-dimensionality of the McMansions now sprawling in the third, fourth and fifth rings of suburbanization will be retrofitted to accommodate social difference and environmental intelligence? What can we learn from migrant neighborhoods about altering our "super-size-me" suburbanization with more sustainable, small-scale social and programmatic adaptations?

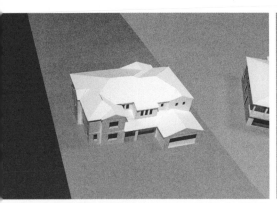
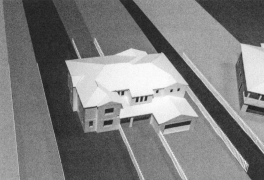

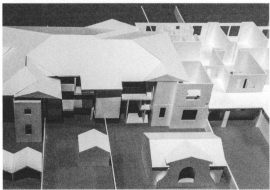

Neighborhood solidarity

Collective practices

Social facilitation

Community capabilities

Survival strategies

Exchange economies

Collaborative uses

Shared property

BUILDING BLOCK

Density = # of Social Exchanges per Area

We are inspired by the everyday urban practices in immigrant neighborhoods, where multigenerational households shape their own micro-economies to maintain a standard for the household, and generate alternative uses and social densities that reshape the fabric of the residential neighborhoods where they settle. Existing mono-use parcels transform through informal economies and densities, neighborhood collaboration and solidaristic social programming. Housing additions in the shape of nonconforming companion units are plugged into existing suburban dwellings to support affordable living configurations. An informal business is launched in a garage; an illegal granny flat is built in the backyard to support an extended family; a shared shed is built straddling the property line between two parcels. We document, visualize and translate these bottom-up adaptations, transactions and negotiations across boundaries and between people and resources to represent social density and advocate for new, more inclusive paradigms of community and economic development.

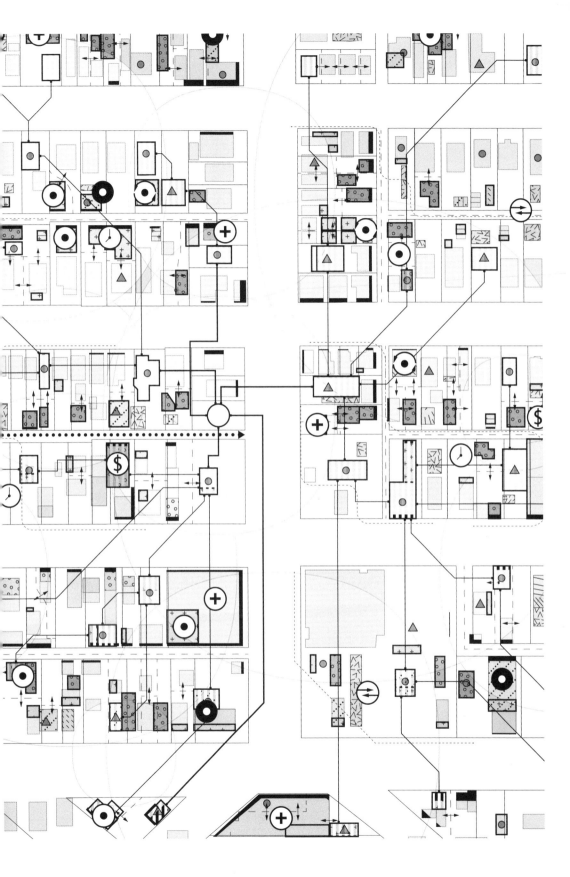

BUILDING BLOCKS

Rethink Ownership

Challenging the "Ownership Society"

Deepening urban inequality and the lack of affordable housing pose profound challenges to the American Dream mythology of private property and home ownership. Even seemingly progressive urban agendas such as *New Urbanism* and the *Creative Class* have resisted fundamental critique of the developer-driven political economy of housing and its profit-oriented bottom line. While New Urbanism retrofits suburbia with a "form-based code" to beautify and urbanize space, with themed facades and corporate superblock in-fill schemes, the ownership models remain exclusionary, unaffordable and monocultural. Similarly, the *Creative Class* agenda has enabled private developers to profit from the urban energies driven by artists and cultural producers without demanding or providing affordable rents for the artists themselves. These neoliberal urban trends have been adopted by municipalities across the US, and have done nothing to rethink existing models of property and affordability. With their facades of "beautification" and their rhetoric of "innovation," both agendas have paved the way to gentrification, and have undermined social and economic inclusion in the city.

14

Retooling Co-ownership

o advances in housing affordability will be achieved hrough design without advances in housing economy nd policy. We need to complicate the meaning of prop- rty and diversify of ownership models, primarily within ones of poverty. We need to prioritize housing as a ollective right and not only as an individual asset that s vulnerable to market speculation. This means devis- ng property models that promote social and racial inte- ration, and that are inclusive of diverse economies of ousing, re-inscribing ownership within an ecology of ublic guarantees. The tools needed to achieve this are lready present, but dormant, within local, state and ederal law. These fragments of legislative history need to be recuperated and re-stitched for new implementa- tions and enforcement. Take, for example, the 1960s Co-op City in the Bronx, which remains the largest middle-in- come affordable housing project in the US, illustrating the potential of United Housing Federations to safeguard long-term affordability. Also consider Community Land Trusts across the country, organized around low-income neighborhoods to ensure community stewardship of lands, property and services to prevent social displace- ments produced by market fluctuation. While many of the best examples, including Co-op City, are still open to examination and criticism, they present generative ideas for reimagining housing affordability in our cities.

Private developers rely on tax credits to ensure profits when developing affordable housing

To qualify for these competitive subsidies, the development typically needs to generate at least 50 units of housing

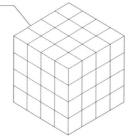

But this kind of density is prohibited by zoning in many mid-city neighborhoods

Little wonder that there is a lack of affordable housing in so many low-income, mid-city neighborhoods

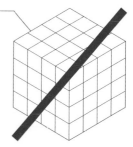

BUILDING BLOCK

Owning the Means of Production

Can communities develop their own housing and public spaces? Can the capacities and economic intelligence of immigrant communities help us redefine established conceptions of ownership? Underserved neighborhoods generate new markets from the bottom up that are typically invisible to conventional top-down urban financing logics. Recognizing and re-evaluating the sweat equity of the local labor in these communities, the entrepreneurial energies and informal economies, can provoke new thinking about ownership and financing. Can we redefine affordability by amplifying the value of community participation? More than "owning" private units, residents, in collaboration with community-based agencies, can generate alternative forms of community property: diverse housing typologies, unconventional community-serving mixed uses, and accessible infrastructures for fabrication and cultural production that incentivize local economy in and for neighborhoods.

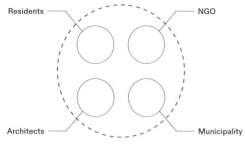

Residents — NGO
Architects — Municipality

A local NGO proposes breaking apart the generic 50-unit project into small buildings, and distributing them throughout the neighborhood

As long as these distributed units are built at the same time and their management is centralized, an NGO can qualify for tax credit based financing, acting as guarantor for the development project

Framed by new social contracts with residents, the NGO works directly with the municipality to prepackage building permits for a portfolio of accessory unit typologies, as well as a microlending structure

Community as Developer

Distributed Community Trusts

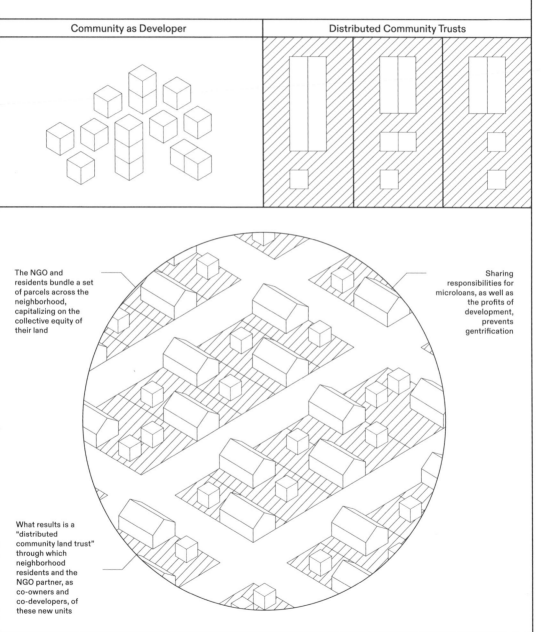

The NGO and residents bundle a set of parcels across the neighborhood, capitalizing on the collective equity of their land

Sharing responsibilities for microloans, as well as the profits of development, prevents gentrification

What results is a "distributed community land trust" through which neighborhood residents and the NGO partner, as co-owners and co-developers, of these new units

BUILDING BLOCKS

Resist Privatization

Reject the Privatization of Everything

Democratizing urban development requires that we question our assumptions about privatization. With the ascendance of neoliberalism since the early 1980s, we have been told that government is an obstacle to markets; that anything public is inefficient, a socialist coup; that regulation is evil, and that to expand our individual economic freedoms we must privatize everything. But there is ample evidence that unchecked privatization of public goods is civic suicide, with direct spatial implications: decimating public investment in infrastructure and dividing the city between zones of wealth and poverty. Greedy privatization is the engine of a vicious cycle through which capital and surplus value bloat the private at the expense of the public. Surplus value itself is not the problem; the problem is that it benefits the few at the expense of the many. The question is how to redirect surplus value to public interests and social priorities, so that communities can benefit from the profits of urbanization. Andrea Skorepa, one of our community activist partners, told us that gentrification itself, when understood as a process of community-directed neighborhood improvement, is not the problem. The problem is when it displaces people, preventing communities from sharing in the profits of their own labor, their own development.

15

The Democratization of Surplus Value

In the early 2000s the city of Medellín, Colombia radically transformed itself from a site of dramatic fragmentation into a model of urban social justice celebrated across the world. Sergio Fajardo, the legendary Mayor who led this transformation, declared that violence is rooted in inequality, and that fighting it required a new civic imagination and concrete investments in public infrastructure and social programs. No city had ever realigned its agendas so effectively and rapidly across sectors, top-down and bottom-up, to invest together in public works. No city had ever entirely reimagined and transformed its own bureaucracy to rapidly mobilize urban interventions on such a massive scale. Medellín demonstrated that government was not the problem but the *solution* when it is modernized and reorganized for agility, transparency and social inclusion. When the world first witnessed Medellín's investments in quality public architecture, public transportation, public space, and public infrastructure investment in the poorest areas of the city, people admired and celebrated the beautiful buildings and projects. But few asked how Medellín managed and paid for it all. We discovered that Medellín had always resisted privatizing its public resources, that it owns telecommunication, water and energy utilities, and reinvests 40% of profits back into public works. In a world seduced by the glimmering mirage of privatization, Medellín's successes provide concrete evidence that spatializing justice through creative public management is still possible.

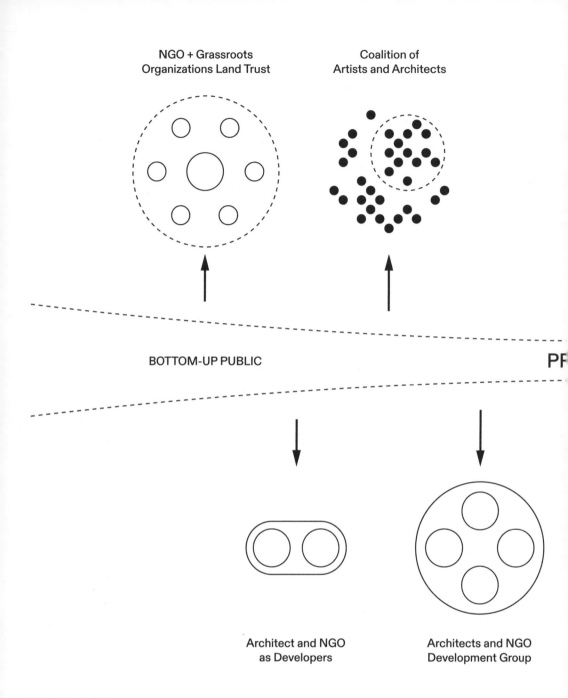

NGO + Grassroots
Organizations Land Trust

Coalition of
Artists and Architects

BOTTOM-UP PUBLIC

PF

Architect and NGO
as Developers

Architects and NGO
Development Group

BUILDING BLOCK

Designing New Social-Economic Coalitions

Fajardo insists that Medellín's transformation was not primarily an architectural project, but a political project to restore social dignity and the primacy of public goods. Essential to this was opening new points of access for community participation in urban development. This entailed democratizing the instruments of economic development across geographies, scales, demographics and the redistribution of surplus value. While we demand, and wait, for a robust top-down public to re-emerge one

day, committed to public investment, progressive taxation and equitable economic development, what do we do in the meantime? We imagine a bottom-up public to perforate the hegemonic horizon of privatization, a million small cuts comprised of cross-sector coalitions at a variety of scales and temporalities that advance inclusion and improve quality of life in local communities most impacted by the forces of exclusion.

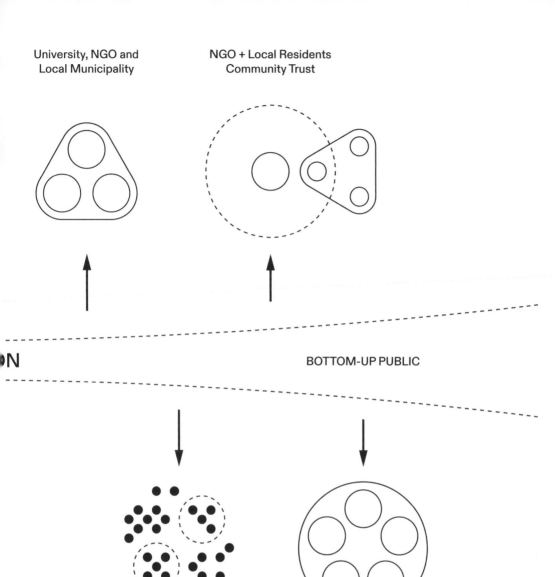

University, NGO and
Local Municipality

NGO + Local Residents
Community Trust

ЭN

BOTTOM-UP PUBLIC

Artists' Collective + Grassroots
Organizations Cooperative

Consortium of
Community-Based Agencies

BUILDING BLOCKS

Demand Generative Zoning

The Apartheid of Everyday Life

It's not that we don't believe in zoning. But why does zoning have to be so stupid? The city of Houston does not have zoning, and yet it has managed to reproduce the backward fragmentation of environments and communities into a suburban archipelago of asphalted islands and big boxes. There is ample history that zoning based on exclusionary land uses leads to segregation by income and race, from the redlining of previous decades to our current debate about preventing denser multi-family affordable housing to challenge sprawl. Zoning prevents inclusive urban development by classifying, categorizing, dividing and segregating, and ultimately producing an apartheid of everyday life. Zoning is frequently discriminatory by design, a scheme to ensure disinvestment, perpetuating the unequal distribution of resources for civic infrastructure, affordable housing and public space, often constructing invisible borders between wealthy white and low-income black and brown communities. But we believe zoning can be recalibrated as an intelligent framework to anticipate social encounter. Zoning is a fruitful site of intervention to choreograph architectures of social propinquity and interdependence, requiring a new political language to spatialize activity and exchange.

16

Visual Prompts for an Anticipatory Zoning

Years ago, urban theorist Stan Allen reminded us that while architects have always been obsessed with the way buildings "look," we should instead focus on what they can "do." In his seminal essay *Field Conditions*, he highlights post-minimalist artists such as Barry Le Va for their interest in process-based dynamics, for designing not deterministic "things" but the conditions within which things can be distributed, managed, and performed.[9]

Barry Le Va's work should be inspirational to urbanists, Allen suggests, for reconceptualizing infrastructure. But for us his sketches are also visual prompts for reimagining zoning. How can these diagrams be translated into new policy language that articulates zoning as a relational scaffold, an anticipatory land-use regulation that can remain flexible, less deterministic and porous?

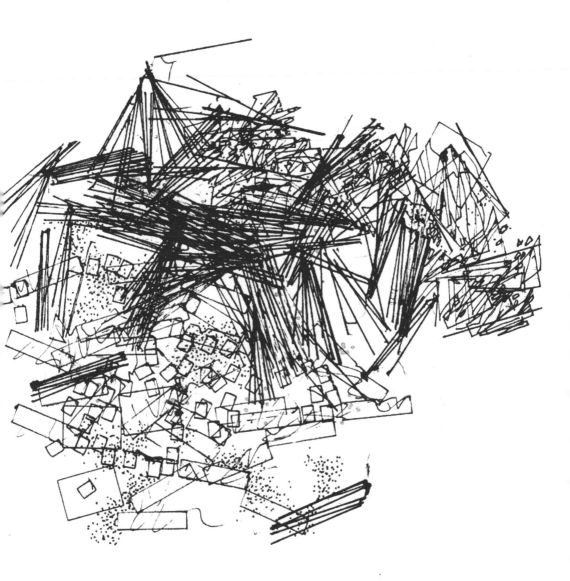

Piercing Blanket Zoning

Zoning must stop being punitive. It must stop preventing socialization. Instead, it should be a generative tool that anticipates, stimulates and organizes social and economic activity at the scale of neighborhoods. This means re-coding the definitions themselves that "give form" to the physical, with enough resilience to absorb unpredictable patterns of everyday life, including: supporting urban-social processes (acknowledging time as design material); incentivizing socio-spatial management, the negotiation between the planned and the unplanned, the invisible social and temporal exchanges found in solidarity, collaboration, informal economy and volunteerism; and adjusting macro-planning through the contingency of the micro to disrupt the homogeneity of "blanket zoning" through irruptions of social difference.

4-2-4 **Interior Lots:** Interior lots (also known as rear lots) may be created if they are in accordance with the following requirements:

    a.   Only one interior lot may be created from a lot of record.

    b.   The interior lot shall have access to a public street, which access shall be no less than thirty (30) feet wide. If the front lot is subdivided to create an interior lot, the front lot shall be required to provide the necessary access to the interior lot.

    c.   Both the front lot and the interior lot must conform to all minimum lot area and other dimensional standards applicable to the zone in which the lots are located, provided, however, that the access strip serving the interior lot shall not be included in computing the minimum lot area for the front and interior lots.

    d.   The front property line of the interior lot shall be deemed to be coincident with the rear property line of the front lot.

4-2-5 **Prohibited Uses:** Except for accessory apartments conforming with the requirements of Section 12-1, or to any other use of a lot expressly permitted by provisions of these regulations, including multifamily use, the following uses of land and buildings are prohibited on private land in all zones:

    a.   Any building for human habitation located to the rear of another building on the same lot.

    b.   Any building for any purpose whatever located in front of any building for human habitation on the same lot.

Section 4-3 **Setbacks**

4-3-1 **Building Setback Standard:** Except as provided in Section 4-3-2 below, all buildings and structures, principal and accessory, shall be located to comply with the minimum and maximum building setbacks established for principal and accessory buildings listed in the zone development standards tables, any supplemental development standards table, condition, or other regulation applicable to the lot or the use being employed at the site.

4-3-2 **Extensions into Required Building Setbacks:**

    a.   **Principal Buildings:**

        Minor Projections Allowed: Minor features of a building such as eaves, chimneys, fire escapes, bay windows, uncovered stairways, wheelchair ramps, and uncovered decks or balconies, may extend into a required Setback up to 20 percent of the setback. Such projection, however, may not extend to within three (3) feet of the lot line.

Mobilize Neighborhoods as Political Units

PROVOCATION

From Cities of Consumption to Neighborhoods of Production

Countering the abstraction of global thinking and the paralysis of governance at national scales, many urban thinkers have focused on the city as the testing ground for more pragmatic and effective modes of intervention, to get things done. But the dramatic privatization and homogenization of city centers in recent years has produced a deficit of new ideas and strategies for equitable urbanization. As urban researchers, thinkers and practitioners regroup to reimagine the city, marginalized neighborhoods would benefit from our focused attention. During the last three decades, while the global city was celebrated as the privileged site for neoliberal consumption and display, neighborhoods at the edges of economic power remained sites of cultural production and economic activity from below, despite dominant discriminatory zoning and economic development. The migrant neighborhood is a reservoir of urban creativity and agency from which to reimagine a new political economy for more inclusive urban development.

17

The Snail Garden: A Cooperative
at the Scale of the Block

In the last years, older neighborhoods in Asian cities have been demolished in order to construct the so called "New Towns." We worked in Anyang, a satellite city outside Seoul, South Korea, on a research project called "Strategies of Coexistence," which focused on some of the neighborhoods slated for demolition. We wanted to challenge the vertical homogeneity of the new tower-developments scheduled to replace these older, horizontal, more heterogeneous mid-density fabrics. While we understood that redeveloping these neighborhoods was inevitable, and necessary to increase density, we opposed the idea of obliterating the existing social-economic relations, local spatial practices and communal forms of governance that defined these environments. While the neighborhoods might "look" obsolete, we discovered behind the facades of worn-out buildings the bottom-up neighborhood dynamics that shaped a complex set of sustainable cooperative economies. We asked: Can these local, solidaristic forms of productivity and governance be protected, fortified and scaled across the New Towns instead of being discarded through a *tabula rasa* approach? The most compelling evidence we found was a snail farm distributed across a city block on five rooftops. The residents blurred their property lines, produced an economic cooperative and a set of protocols for local management. Their neighborhood block became an alternative political and economic unit that produced sustainable revenue and a culture of neighborhood solidarity.

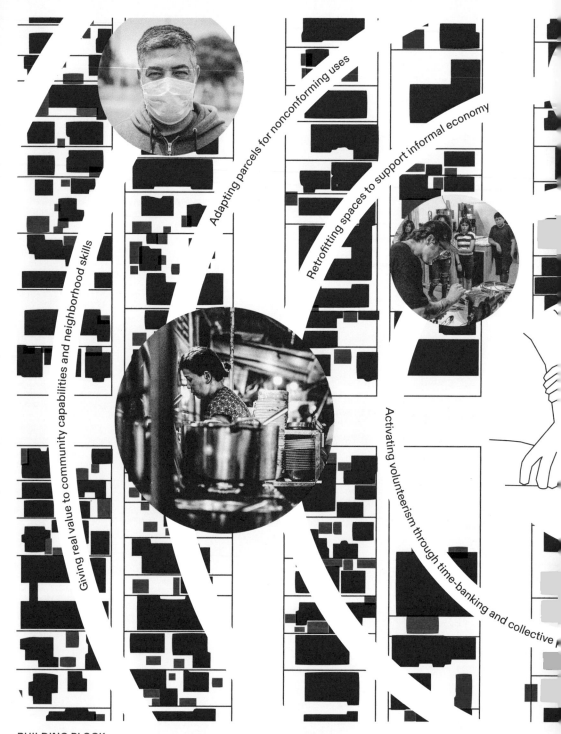

Giving real value to community capabilities and neighborhood skills

Adapting parcels for nonconforming uses

Retrofitting spaces to support informal economy

Activating volunteerism through time-banking and collective

BUILDING BLOCK

"Bundling" Bottom-Up Practices

Our work focuses on the micro-scale of the border neighborhood as an urban laboratory from which to begin restitching a new civic imagination and advocating for policies that protect and fortify bottom-up productivity and governance. For us, this means partnering with community-based agencies to document local modes of production, bundling cultural, social, economic and political practices to reimagine housing and infrastructure at the scale of parcels, blocks and neighborhoods.

Spatializing the intensity of solidaristic social programming

ularizing needs with incremental additions and flexible uses

Negotiating property lines to share infrastructure

Summoning activist and participatory energies with coalitions of care

Validate Everyday Work

Restoring the Social Value of Labor

COVID-19 exposed our collective dependence on frontline workers, who ensured a steady supply of essential goods and services while many of us were holed-up safely in our private retreats. These low-wage workers risked their lives, returning home each day to vulnerable communities disproportionately ravaged by sickness and unnecessary death. And to this day they remain underappreciated, undercompensated, and marginalized in public policy, formally denied a guaranteed living wage. Instead of a social safety net, our neoliberal illusion touts the joyful independence of the "gig economy," selling the idea of worker autonomy through "flex time" and being one's own boss. We have abandoned the working class in America, eroded the social safety net, and the protection of labor rights. The history of alienated labor marches on, with a healthy dose of false consciousness leading many to align politically against their own best interests, and yet the worker's productive life in America is devoted to expanding the profits of others.

Work should manifest the capacities and desires of the worker, and workers should benefit directly from the fruits of their labor. Labor should also construct local community and organize social relations of productivity. Architects and urban designers committed to spatializing justice should ensure, at minimum, that they are not through their work bolstering political economies of labor exploitation. More proactively, we can mobilize our unique skills and capacities to co-develop neighborhood infrastructures of productivity with marginalized communities that enable local residents to imagine new individual and collective economic pathways, to own and manage the means of production, and ultimately to benefit directly from their own labor.

18

Feminist Architectures

Our social norms and behaviors, labor practices and the spatial evolution of the city itself are grounded in patriarchal structures that have always thrived through gender subordination and exclusion. In the 1990s, Catalan theorist Ignasi de Solà-Morales described the "Terrain Vague," leftovers after the flattening of space by the bulldozers of development, that reverberated our estrangement from ourselves, exiled and marginalized from the official circuits of consumption. He invited architects to engage these spaces with a different sensibility, less top-down, colonizing and patriarchal, and more nomadic, ecological and performative—a *queer sensibility*, as architecture critic Aaron Betsky would later call it. Gender is implicitly inscribed in architecture: it can spatialize exclusionary power and social control; or it can summon inclusion, sociability and encounter. Social utopian feminist activists

and thinkers at the end of the 19th century, such as Charlotte Perkins Gilman (of the *Feminist Apartment Hotel*) and Melusina Fay Pierce (of *Cooperative Housekeeping*), engaged the social value of labor and its spatial consequences, elevating domestic labor (the kitchen, the laundry, the nursery) as the engine for new cohousing communities and a new neighborhood-scale cooperative economy. So too Alice Constance Austin, who in the early 20th century proposed the *Llano del Rio*, a cooperative that centralized kitchens, laundries and daycare to emancipate women from the isolation of domestic toil. They all envisioned communities of collectivized labor, reorganizing social and economic relations to counter labor inequality and patriarchal household protocols, and align diverse capacities around common spaces.

BUILDING BLOCKS

Re-collectivizing the Kitchen

The majority of community-based social agencies across the world are led by women, whose anti-patriarchal sensibilities advance civic leadership based on empathy, inclusion, and curatorial protocols of mediation and facilitation. Communal kitchens, too, spatialize an eco-feminist imagination for urban justice. As social infrastructure, they are designed to generate solidaristic political subjectivities of emancipation, self-management and a shared economy; and when they are connected to

urban farming, inter-generational learning spaces, community programming and local economic steward-ship, communal kitchens can become powerful engines for local social change, linking social, environmental and food justice with entrepreneurship and small-scale economic development. They become an important paradigm for mixed and collective housing configura-tions in underserved, low-income neighborhoods.

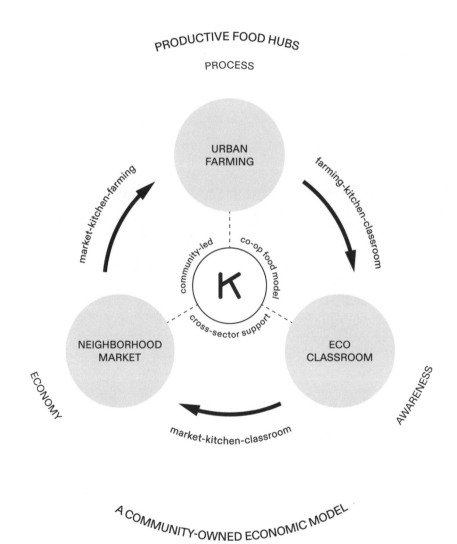

PRODUCTIVE FOOD HUBS

PROCESS

URBAN FARMING

market-kitchen-farming

farming-kitchen-classroom

community-led

co-op food model

K

cross-sector support

NEIGHBORHOOD MARKET

ECO CLASSROOM

ECONOMY

AWARENESS

market-kitchen-classroom

A COMMUNITY-OWNED ECONOMIC MODEL

Community kitchen generates socialization

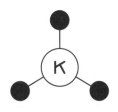

Co-op kitchen, shared community asset

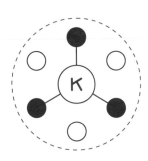

Social housing units embedded in collective kitchens co-managed by residents

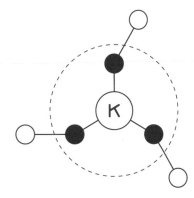

Senior housing threaded by collective kitchens and food programs

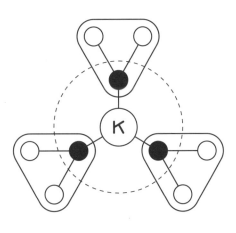

Urban farming, food-hubs, civic classrooms, and business entrepreneurship synergized by communal kitchen incubators

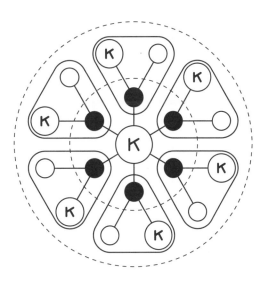

An infrastructure of small kitchens under one roof shape a neighborhood food market led by local residents

Intervene in the Developer's Proforma

Appropriating the Knowledge of the Developer

The developer's proforma contains the mathematics for any architectural intervention in the city. It is the spreadsheet that lists (soft) project expenses, (hard) construction costs, lending structures and development revenues, whose bottom line is maximizing profit for the developer. The developer's proforma precedes architecture. It is the financial envelope that eventually gives form to the building, articulating its programmatic priorities and construction typologies. In a sense, the developer's proforma is architecture's *financial plastic*. The monopoly of urban development through the economic logics of this spreadsheet have incited us to steal the developer's knowledge, tools and procedures. The ability to mobilize his equity capacity in order to manipulate resources (cheap lending) and time (narrowing the time between loan-award and certificate of occupancy, so that rents repay the loan without him spending his own equity) is a perfect equation that yields minimum investment for maximum profit. We as architects and urban designers can intervene in the organizational and financial strategies of the developer's spreadsheet in order to redistribute resources, spatialize inclusion and socialize profit.

19

AQUISITION COSTS

Land cost	132,605	$ 5^{00}	663,025		
	ft²	$/ft²	$		
				663,025	

CONSTRUCTION COSTS

Construction	ft²	Rate ft²	Cost		
Mixed-use development	60,000	$ 100^{00}	6,000,000		
Contingency		10,00%	600,000		
Offsite improvements	81,000 ft²	81,000 ft²	972,000		
				1,572,000	

TI COSTS

TI cost area rate					
Mixed use			2,800,000		
				2,800,000	

PROFESSIONAL FEES

$$15\% \; X = Y$$

Construction Cost ——— Architect's Sweat Equity

Architect & Engineering: 15% of architect co...			757,200		
Architecture			412,200		
Title 24 consultant			10,000		
Structural engineer					
Acoustical engineer					
Soils engineer					
Appraisal					
Plans / Permits			110,000		
Permits and fees			105,000		
Blueprints			5,000		
Legal			57,000		
Appraisal			6,250		
Inspections			6,000		
Environmental review			2,000		
Soft costs contingency			400,000		
Operating expenses during construction			40,000		

Activating the Hidden Value of "Sweat Equity"

Legendary San Diego architect Ted Smith reminds us that architects can become developers of their own projects. Our services as architects in the US amount to 15% of a project's construction costs, and this *under-capitalized asset* can be mobilized as collateral for development. Now imagine, he suggested, if we were to collaborate with other architects, pooling resources to buy a small piece of land, and perhaps summoning a couple of consultants as partners (primarily structural engineers, whose services amount to 8–10% of the construction costs). The cost of the land, plus the value of our collective sweat equity as architect-developers, amounts to enough collateral to qualify for boiler-plate lending. This idea that architects can take control of urban development has transformed San Diego in the last years into a laboratory for architect-led development. The Bault-Groupen in Berlin, Germany is similar, where small coalitions of architects pooled their resources and sweat equity to develop their own flats, including other rentals to generate income for themselves and sustain their own practices. Nothing should prevent us architects and artists from becoming developers of our own projects and partnering with communities in the process.

(Re)presenting informal economy	Collective forms of land acquisition
(participation has value)	(co-owning parcels)
New political representation	Architects' sweat equity
(architect as translator of social value)	(fees as collateral)
Consultants' sweat equity	Social impact investment
(fees as collateral)	(redirecting philanthropic equity)
Community trusts	Foundation investment
(co-developing with communities)	(grants as seed money)
New lending representation	Activating subsidies for community-serving uses
(i.e., Public universities as guarantors of leases)	(i.e., New Market Tax Credits)

BUILDING BLOCK

Socializing the Developer's Proforma: Bundling Sweat Equity

While these efforts illustrate the power of architects to democratize the tools and knowledge of development, the profits generated by these experiments remain private. The question is how we can transfer this creative knowledge to low-income communities. We have asked: Can the developer's spreadsheet be appropriated and deployed to construct community, where diverse, under-valued forms of labor can produce new mechanisms for urban and economic development?

Can we synergize the sweat equity of architects, the equity of local NGOs, the hidden value of informal economy, neighborhood participation and collaboration?

As architects, can we also act as facilitators, to translate, represent and integrate the value of this bottom-up labor into a new model of shared urban development? By mobilizing the operational dimension of social and economic agency we can curate new partners to transform the developer's spreadsheet into a social engine for community-based development. The sweat equity of architects, cultural producers and community leaders; the economic equity of public universities; and municipal protocols for accessing public parcels can be aggregated to enable communities to develop their own neighborhoods. This has been our story.

AQUISITION COSTS					
Land cost					
CONSTRUCTION COSTS					
Construction					
Mixed-use development					
Contingency					
Offsite improvements					
TI COSTS					
TI cost area rate					
Mixed use					
PROFESSIONAL FEES					
Architect & Engineering: 10% of direct cost					
Architecture					
Title 24 consultant					
Structural engineer					
Acoustical engineer					
Soils engineer					
Appraisal					
Plans / Permits					
Permits and fees					
Blueprints					
Legal					
Appraisal					
Inspections					
Environmental review					
Soft costs contingency					
Operating expenses during construction					
Financial					
Loan fees					
Loan signing fee					
Contingency					
TOTAL COST					
TOTAL COST + INTEREST AND FEES					
Interest paid for debt sources:					
Construction loan (7.50%)					
Total interest paid for debt sources					

Co-develop with Communities

Developing the City with "Others"

Within the neoliberal political economy of urban development, the profits of urbanization are privatized and drive the financialization of almost every sector of the built environment. The private developer is the main actor in this closed system of capital accumulation, monopolizing the means of urban production as well as the knowledge for accessing the economic tools for redevelopment. Often, this monopoly of resources and knowledges is supported by private-public partnerships, through which public subsidies endorse private interests at the expense of public priorities. Underserved communities are left out of these equations. But can a community be a developer, and be integrated into urban processes to co-produce the city? Can new alliances between community-based organizations and municipalities provide more inclusive access to public lands for development? Can large public institutions (universities, hospitals, schools, museums) partner with communities to promote neighborhood-based productivity and job-generation? Can architects and communities collaborate to produce a new economic model for small-scale urban development?

20

What Do We Do While Waiting for
the Urban Revolution to Arrive?

Our research on informal urbanization, through which left-over spaces are made productive by bottom-up practices of adaptation, resonates with Henri Lefebvre's aspiration to revolutionize everyday life through the spatialization of social relations of production. But most of this stealth urban energy has not yet trickled upward to detonate a more pervasive urban revolution, transforming the city through collective demands for social democratic values, meanings, exchanges and spaces. Instead of waiting for the urban revolution to arrive, let's declare it already here and work to incrementally scale-up these informal acts of community development. Let's build new coalitions for inclusive urban development, led by communities, and find inspiration in their bottom-up praxis of informal economy and labor.

BUILDING BLOCKS

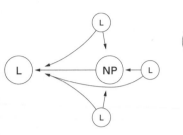

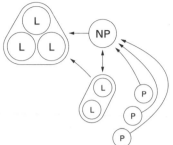

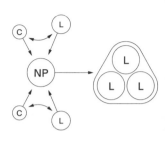

Scenario 1

NGO owns land and develops
over time

Scenario 2

NGO bundles land with community
participants and co-develops over time

Scenario 3

NGO mediates coalition of participants
to bundle capital and purchase land

BUILDING BLOCK

Protocols for Shared Urbanization

When we assign value to the skills and capabilities of informal urbanization, and aggregate this hidden value with the sweat equity of architects, cultural producers, and community leaders, and finally connect these assets to the resources of public institutions, including new municipal protocols for accessing public parcels, THIS is the leverage communities need to co-develop the city.

The possibility of community-led urban develoment can be accelerated by: identifying the programmatic and social capital of non-profits and residents as "recognizable" assets; partnering with architects and harnessing the value of their sweat equity for project development; mobilizing the programmatic and economic power of universities as leverage for communities to develop their own public spaces and affordable housing; and redirecting the purchase power of public institutions from corporations to communities to support the development of new cooperative, revenue-generating business models owned by communities.

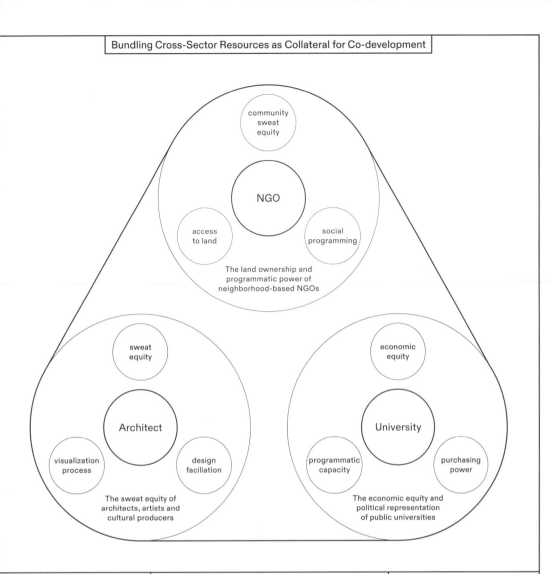

community
sweat
equity

NGO

access
to land

social
programming

The land ownership and
programmatic power of
neighborhood-based NGOs

sweat
equity

Architect

visualization
process

design
faciliation

The sweat equity of
architects, artists and
cultural producers

economic
equity

University

programmatic
capacity

purchasing
power

The economic equity and
political representation
of public universities

Municipal Protocols for Accessing Public Parcels

Co-development model with communities = bundled assets + land equity

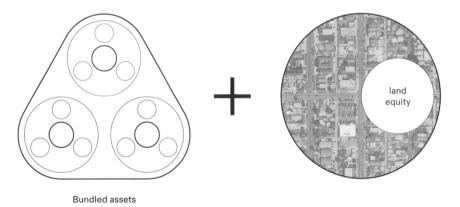

land
equity

Bundled assets

Transform Housing Beyond "Units"

PROVOCATION

In Conditions of Poverty, "Units" Cannot Exist on Their Own

The crisis of housing affordability is a local, national and global problem. This crisis will continue as long as housing is understood as a commodity, an object of profit, vulnerable to the fluctuation of free markets and discriminatory public policies. Also problematic from the vantage point of equity is the normative understanding of housing as autonomous "units" that lack the social infrastructure necessary to sustain them—a function of the commercialization and financialization of urban development. In the US, calling affordable housing "public" or "social" would amount to condemning it as a de facto ghetto. In many countries across the world housing is called *public* or *social* because it is managed by the state, which in conditions of inequality guarantees what markets will not: protecting housing from real estate speculation and inflation, regulating against segregation, monopoly and homogenization, and assuring affordability and inclusion as a right. For progressive societies, affordable housing is not stigmatized, polarized and criminalized, but elevated as generative urban infrastructure, a tool for integration and collective social and economic equity.

21

Pruitt-Igoe was Not Evil

When Pruitt-Igoe was built in Saint Louis, Missouri in the beginning of the 1950s, it was exemplary of New Deal public housing. By the beginning of the 1970s it had devolved into a violent ghetto. The famous image of Pruitt-Igoe's demolition in the late 1970s generated two American myths: first, as perpetuated by historian Charles Jencks, that modern architecture was responsible for Pruitt-Igoe's demise; the other, that public housing was dead in the US, moving the discussion from hyper-public to hyper-private. Both myths demonized public housing and caused irreparable damage to the city. The real causes of Pruitt-Igoe's decline must be exposed as part of our housing debate. When Pruitt-Igoe was built its housing units thrived. They were equipped with social, economic and educational support systems enabled by progressive taxation and social policies. When those support systems eroded with time, and the units were left to their own devices, Pruitt-Igoe rapidly imploded.

BUILDING BLOCKS

BUILDING BLOCK

Embedding Social Housing in Infrastructures of Support

Housing must not be understood as a collection of independent units, but as part of an integral framework for social integration and economic sustainability. In other words, in conditions of poverty housing units cannot stand alone; they need to be embedded in an infrastructure of social, economic and cultural support. This includes flexible social and pedagogical spaces, economic incubators coordinated by local community agencies, and curated by cross-sector coalitions to inject funding, resources and management to assure sustainable social and economic relations. Transforming affordable housing from autonomous units into relational social systems transforms housing into neighborhood infrastructure, an economic catalyst for job generation and the development of new forms of sociability, solidarity, and inclusion.

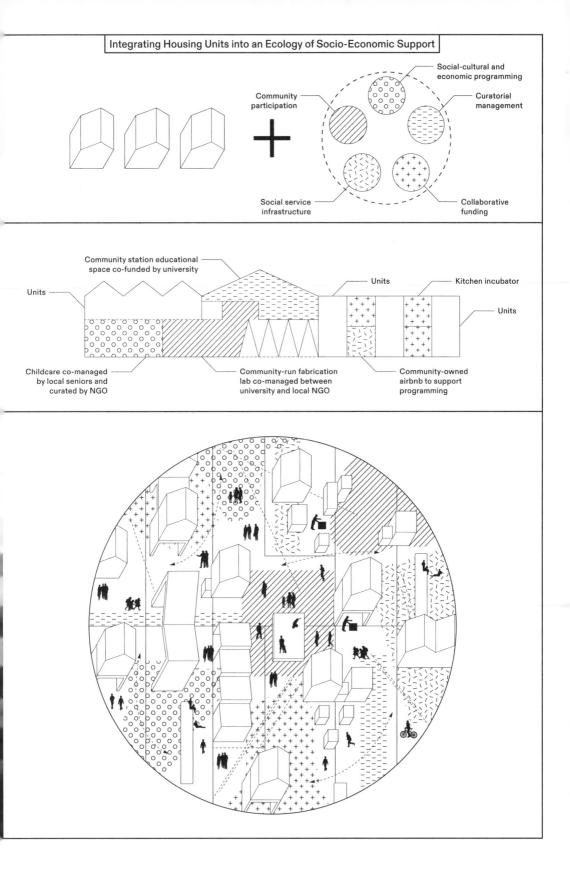

Integrating Housing Units into an Ecology of Socio-Economic Support

Community participation

Social-cultural and economic programming

Curatorial management

Collaborative funding

Social service infrastructure

Units

Community station educational space co-funded by university

Units

Kitchen incubator

Units

Childcare co-managed by local seniors and curated by NGO

Community-run fabrication lab co-managed between university and local NGO

Community-owned airbnb to support programming

BUILDING BLOCKS

Transcend Hospitality

From Hospitality to Inclusion

It is urgent today that we reassert a global ethical commitment to hospitality to the "stranger in distress," and to intervene at the sites of first contact between the nation and the other: *the host city*. Migrants arriving from places ravaged by war, persecution and poverty have immediate needs for food and water, medicine and shelter. Addressing these needs is the proper charitable response of an ethical society. In other words, hospitality is the first gesture, an essential charitable opening, a first step in creating a more inclusive and welcoming society. But as needs become more complex over time, charity is not the appropriate model for building an inclusive society. We need to expand the meaning of hospitality into inclusion, and this demands transformation in the spatial and programmatic arrangements of the host city. Inclusion means integrating the migrant and her children into social, economic and political life, creating spaces for meaningful community participation, and opportunities for education, psychological and spiritual health. Real inclusion is more than a hospitable embrace; it is a process through which we ourselves transform alongside the other.

22

The Right to Migrate, the Right to Remain, the Right to Return

Between 2016 and 2020, San Diego-Tijuana became the main site of arrival for thousands of Central American and Haitian immigrants seeking asylum in the US. While many of them waited at the wall for court hearings that never came, repelled with tear gas by US border patrol agents, reviled by the Mexican public as a nuisance, a drain on scarce public resources, hundreds of migrants were forced to find refuge in makeshift camps distributed in the interstices of the city, or in the informal settlements at the periphery. In this period of accelerating migration, we often hear about the rights of immigrants to flee political persecution, violence, and extreme poverty. But in Tijuana, where many migrants were denied access to the US but could not return safely to their own countries, we must also consider the "right to remain," the right to belong. Our geopolitical reality in the border zone has pushed us to reflect on intersections of migrant rights and the rights to the city, and what it means to think in an infrastructural way about moving from hospitality to inclusion. Zones of refuge cannot be understood only as temporary shelters located in the interstices or at the margins of cities, but must be integrated more deliberately into the metropolitan fabric.

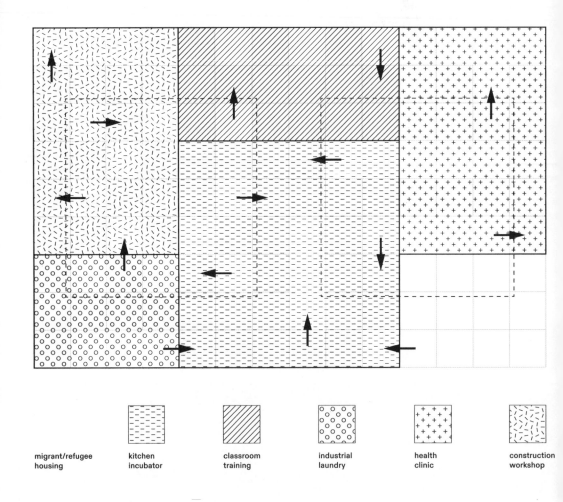

migrant/refugee housing

kitchen incubator

classroom training

industrial laundry

health clinic

construction workshop

BUILDING BLOCK

From Ephemeral Habitation to Incremental Permanency

Just as climate change is forcing us to reimagine the city as a more porous and resilient urban-ecological system, unprecedented migration summons us to adapt the city into a more flexible framework to anticipate social emergency, inclusion and integration. "Thinking beyond shelter" means rethinking refugee camps everywhere, from places of short-term habitation and service provision to durable infrastructure for inclusion. Inscribed within a sanctuary economy for productivity and self-reliance, migrant shelters can be agile infrastructures that support and anticipate both transition and rootedness, the ephemeral and the permanent.

SANCTUARY COMMUNITY TRUST

Activist-led Refugee Camp, Tijuana

A. Community Ownership

1. Activist NGO organization
2. Immigrant-refugee community representation
3. Rotating coordinating committee led by NGO

B. University-Led Cross-Sector Coalition

4. Educational and social service programming and training
5. Political representation and facilitation
6. Educational investments

C. Social-Economic Incubators

7. Kitchen incubator
8. Classroom training
9. Industrial laundry
10. Health clinic
11. Construction workshop

D. Economic Model

Refugee Camp Construction Cooperative (Community Owned)

12. Seed Monies / Community-University Cross-Sector Coalition

    - Land acquisition (seed loan)
    - Migrant shares (sweat equity and time banking)
    - Seed investors (no-interest loans by foundations)
    - Municipal subsidy for local rehab projects
    - Foundation and philanthropic grants
    - Social-impact seed loan
    - Industry (subsidized materials and grants)

13. Expenses + Revenue

    - Workers' salary
    - Management
    - Investor repay
    - Profits and reserve funds

14. Investments

    - Social programs
    - Job training
    - Community development
    - Local infrastructure

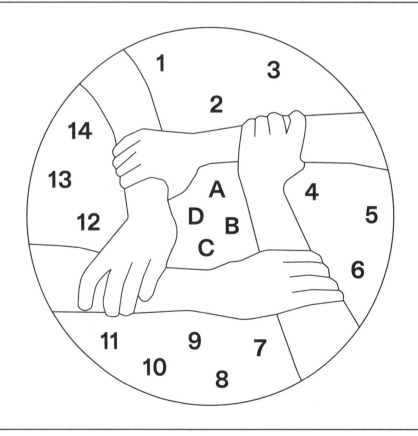

BUILDING BLOCKS

Democratize Access

Unwalling Space

Border walls physicalize an urbanization of fear. While they are designed to partition territories, they are invisibly reproduced across the city. No-loitering legislation has walled public space into a rigid field of criminality and social profiling, preventing flexibility of use and urban expression. Gigantic shopping malls camouflage themselves as public space but perform as securitized private spaces for consumption. Themed environments and urban policies of beautification become exclusionary by default, rejecting those who appear not to "belong," while gated communities partition the urban field, overtly walling themselves into private fortresses. Instead of democratizing knowledge, algorithmic regimes have sedimented disinformation platforms, splintering cyberspace into walled monocultures characterized by polarization and hatred. Protectionist urbanization divides the urban and the environmental, flattening nature to wall the ecological. And for citizens in wheelchairs, a 6" curve is an unsurmountable border wall, as are all architectures that deny access to people with diverse abilities. Spatializing justice demands that we urgently democratize access.

23

She Sat Where She Did Not Belong

An emblematic image of the US Civil Rights movement is Rosa Parks sitting where she did not belong. Even though the bus was "public," it was not accessible to many. This apartheid of the "public" is not as overt today as it was then. Today privatization has naturalized exclusion, making all spaces "neutral" and ambiguously public. To guarantee concrete urban rights of access we need to reject naïve conceptions of "public," and recognize the duplicity of the private. Occupying the seat of her oppressor, Rosa Parks certainly challenged overt racism. But in that act, she was also demanding access to all urban spaces and processes. Her "sit-in" claimed urban mobility as a human right, but also made great strides toward dissolving obstacles to inclusion and demanding institutional transparency and accountability.

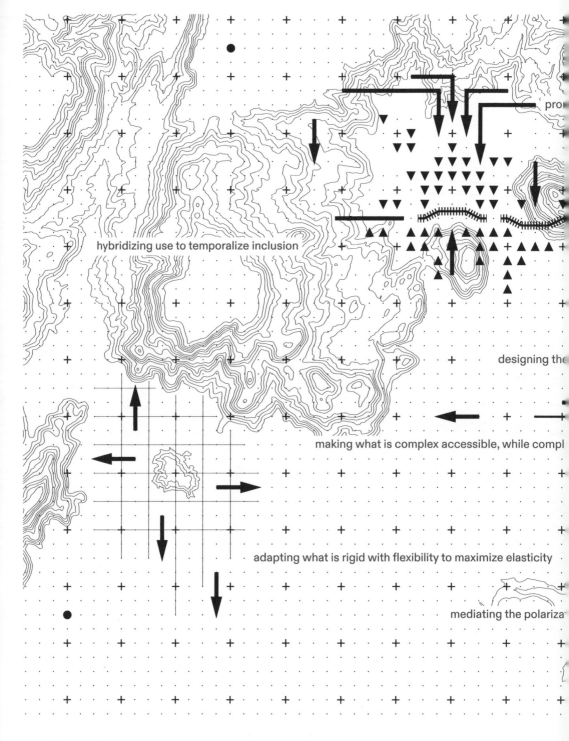

hybridizing use to temporalize inclusion

pro

designing the

making what is complex accessible, while compl

adapting what is rigid with flexibility to maximize elasticity

mediating the polariza

BUILDING BLOCK

Designing the Rights of Entry

Spatial justice demands more of architects than designing beautiful spaces in the city. We must also design
access and the protocols that assure inclusion. In this
sense, democratizing the city means democratizing

access, flow and mobility through specific urban and
policy design strategies that maximize flexibility, adapt-
ability, porosity and diversity.

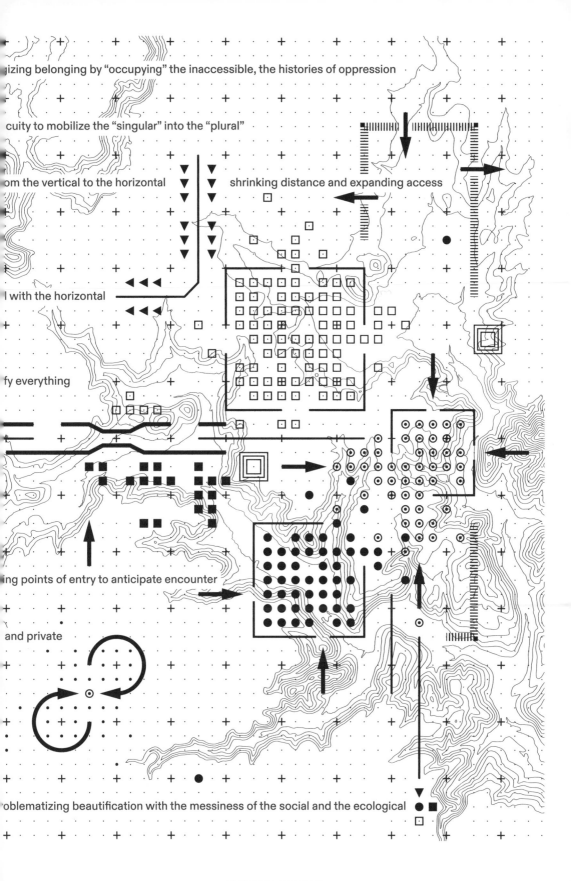

izing belonging by "occupying" the inaccessible, the histories of oppression

cuity to mobilize the "singular" into the "plural"

om the vertical to the horizontal   shrinking distance and expanding access

l with the horizontal

fy everything

ing points of entry to anticipate encounter

and private

oblematizing beautification with the messiness of the social and the ecological

Activate Public Space

Public Space Constructs Citizen Culture

Urban justice demands that we question our conventional conceptions of public space and rethink its civic function in the city. Existing misconceptions about public space include: 1. that a nicely designed plaza, with the right benches and shade, will magically ensure socialization and inclusion; 2. that flanking public space with reliable commercial franchises to expand traffic and flow and expensive housing developments will achieve economic sustainability; and in the worst of scenarios 3. that filling residual space on a map at the planning office with green-colored markers will transform open space into public space. The first paradigm emerges from our obsession with beautification at the expense of inclusion and civic participation; the second from our faith in the market and the commodification, privatization and branding of the public realm; and the third from a faulty planning tradition that remains neutral in its designation of public space as "undifferentiated space" without any connection to civic priorities. All of these paradigms need to be questioned, as they all invite social and economic exclusion—and this includes the "sponsored" temporary pop-ups that turn our public spaces into sites of leisure and consumption. They too often accelerate gentrification, appropriate arts and culture for private ends, and become an apology for the absence of more substantial public investment in the city. Public space should instead be rearticulated as the civic infrastructure of the city, to mobilize a robust citizenship culture.

24

Spatializing Citizenship in Medellín

When mathematician Sergio Fajardo became Mayor in 2005, he committed to transforming Medellín into "the most educated" city in Colombia. In the aftermath of the world's most notorious drug war, he insisted that violence limits opportunities, and that knowledge and social inclusion open them. He declared that public space should become a priviliged site, where new civic possibilities can be understood, experienced and mobilized. This entailed a deliberate process of desiging long-term institutional support and programming for public spaces,

to ensure inclusion and long-term civic impact. This vision manifested most clearly in Fajardo's famous *Library Parks* project, built strategically in the poorest, most vulnerable informal settlements in the periphery of the city. The Library Parks are "public spaces that educate," where physical design was accompanied by cross-sector curatorial management, programming and resources to promote sustainable civic education, cultural production and small-scale economic development. Public space spatializes citizenship.

Designing Spaces and Protocols Together

Designing inclusive public spaces involves curating architectures that spatialize citizenship, transforming often passive public spaces into flexible and adaptable sites for the co-production of knowledge and local economy. This means designing physical spaces and the protocols for inclusion simultaneously. We believe public space must become civilized, to use James Tully's beautiful concept—a site of dialogue and contestation, and infused with resources and tools to increase public knowledge and community capacity for political and environmental action.[11]

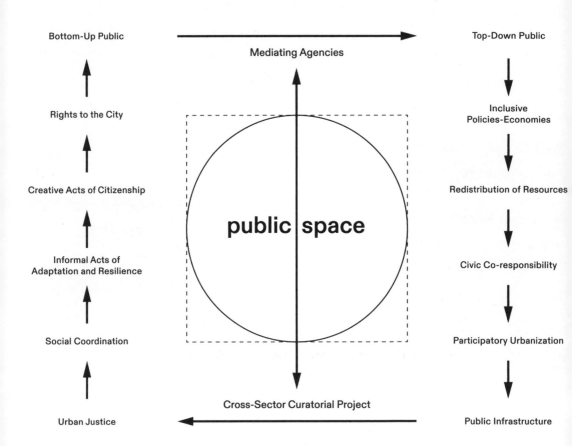

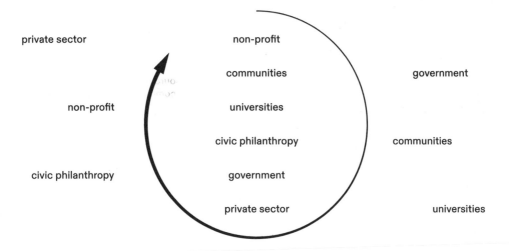

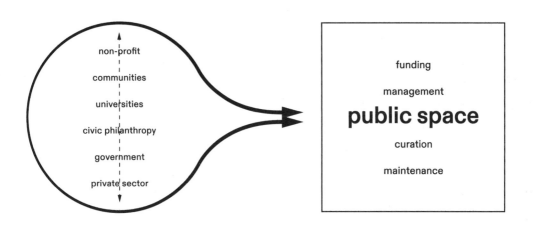

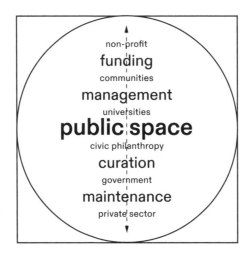

BUILDING BLOCKS

Curate New Urban Pedagogies

Increasing Public Knowledge: Problematizing Advocacy Planning

We are critical of generic municipal "advocacy planning" methods, which too often collude with the agendas of private developers rather than represent community priorities. Community planning workshops tend to focus on architectural style, mobilizing consensus by "packaging identity" through aesthetics, rather than increasing community awareness and meaningful participation by visualizing the policy conditions that have prevented equitable social and economic development. Community-based planning workshops need to penetrate the contested space between top-down and bottom-up assumptions and clichés. It is not enough to ask low-income communities what they want, without providing the tools, the evidence, the references, the visualizations, the histories that can provoke more imaginative, critical thinking about what is possible, about what development can mean for their neighborhood, and the economic opportunities that might be foreclosed by the options placed before them. In other words, participatory planning requires critical dialogical processes, organized around common issues of concern, through which the specialized design strategies of planners and architects and the activist intelligence of communities can intersect to generate new public knowledge.

25

Bogotá's "Citizenship Cards"

Spatializing justice requires new strategies of public communication, new urban pedagogies to challenge anti-democratic biases and misinformation that sow civic mistrust in the urban political process and lead citizens to withdraw, or to vote against their own interests. Inheriting a 20th-century lineage of Latin American civic experimentation and urban pedagogy, Bogotá's legendary mayor, philosopher Antanas Mockus (1995–97; 2001–03) curated public performances that intervened in dysfunctional social norms and a profound lack of social recognition among the citizens of Bogotá. Mockus's *citizenship culture* interventions were grounded in a belief that urban transformation is as much about changing social norms and behavior, and patterns of public trust and social cooperation from the bottom up, as it is about progressive urban, public health and environmental policy from the top down. During his administration, Mockus summoned artists and cultural producers to help mobilize a cohesive civic identity through participatory cultural action to change hearts and minds through performative pedagogical tactics that intervened in everyday social relations. These cultural interventions included replacing hundreds of corrupt traffic police with a troupe of mimes who shamed pedestrians for jaywalking and drivers for endangering pedestrians. Another intervention involved distributing *citizenship cards* depicting a "thumbs-up" and "thumbs-down" that were employed by citizens in their daily interactions to express approval or disapproval of each other's behavior. Through this repeated performative game of mutual recognition, citizens were deciding together the kind of city they wished to inhabit and how to enforce these aspirations collectively.

Designing Community Processes

Mockus demonstrated that social, moral and legal norms can be recalibrated and reoriented at the urban scale through top-down municipal intervention in community processes. In contexts of extreme public violence and social rupture, law-and-order solutions do not work because they don't internalize new values. Instead, Mockus expanded the role of art as a tool for community engagement, and new collaborative forms of governance and civic participation. His legacy continues to inspire us to design new, more transgressive strategies of civic education and critical methods for advocacy planning, including the design of visual tools that expose the injustice, illuminate interdependencies, demonstrate the virtues of solidarity, and stimulate a new civic imagination. Can we design new community processes to disrupt the cultural transmission and practice of racism, xenophobia, classism, ableism, sexism and homophobia in our cities? Can we design a new citizenship culture?

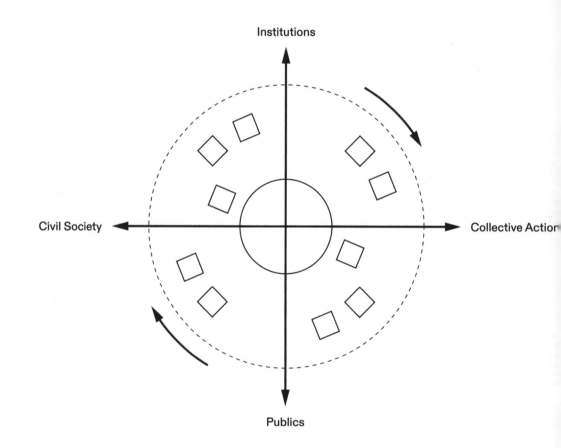

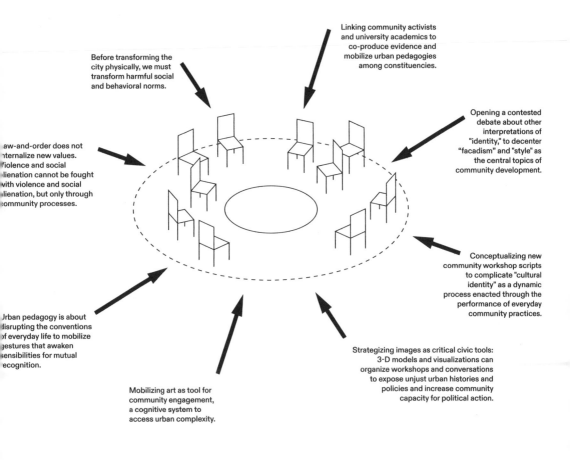

TOP-DOWN

Recalibrating norms

Legal	Moral	Social

Before transforming the city physically, we must transform harmful social and behavioral norms.

Linking community activists and university academics to co-produce evidence and mobilize urban pedagogies among constituencies.

Opening a contested debate about other interpretations of "identity," to decenter "facadism" and "style" as the central topics of community development.

Law-and-order does not internalize new values. Violence and social alienation cannot be fought with violence and social alienation, but only through community processes.

Conceptualizing new community workshop scripts to complicate "cultural identity" as a dynamic process enacted through the performance of everyday community practices.

Urban pedagogy is about disrupting the conventions of everyday life to mobilize gestures that awaken sensibilities for mutual recognition.

Strategizing images as critical civic tools: 3-D models and visualizations can organize workshops and conversations to expose unjust urban histories and policies and increase community capacity for political action.

Mobilizing art as tool for community engagement, a cognitive system to access urban complexity.

Shifting from the vertical to the horizontal is an ethical move

BOTTOM-UP

BUILDING BLOCKS

Civicize Platforms

Challenging the Algorithmic Regime

Platforms reflect technology's historic double identity, simultaneously utopian and dystopian, a tool for both social emancipation and control. Digital social platforms can be understood as a commons, a collective resource for democratizing information, a summoner of activist practices to support human rights and increase our capacities for social transformation. But they can also be instruments of social control, brilliantly organized within an algorithmic regime through which we become mediated bubbles of phantasmagoric sociability. The profiteers of social media platforms feed on social fragmentation, alienation and polarization, and relativizing truth through misinformation. In this sense, digital platforms are the apotheosis of neoliberalism —an unregulated field, where neutral, unrestricted choice and opportunistic exploitation make everything possible, surreptitiously encroaching into our lives to harvest our private angsts and desires, our public needs and pleasures, only to monetize them as transactional data. We must not mistake the "commons" for an ambiguous, open-ended collective resource framework, lacking social constraints, concrete ethical mandates and organizational structures for the protection of collective and individual rights. Devoid of public protections, platforms will always be appropriated by the algorithmic seductions and deathtraps of digital capitalism.

26

The Tragedy of the Commons Redux

Superstudio's *The Continuous Monument* and *Super-surface* are two of the most powerful images of the postwar European architectural *avant-garde*. Again, simultaneously utopian and dystopian, they anticipated the internet as a "commons of availabilities," a platform upon which nomadic communities could construct their architecture-less socio-spatial relations through the exchange of knowledges and resources. Organized by the simultaneity of local and global affinities, they also represented a dystopian critique of the architecture of sameness enveloping the globe, embracing a homogenizing consumerist culture at the expense of local idiosyncrasy and difference. For us, real communities collaged inside the abstract grid have always suggested rituals of resistance, piercing the blanket of conformity with everyday acts of sociability. These images also anticipate the conflicting destinies of digital platforms, what we might think of as a "tragedy of the digital commons"—a reservoir of limitless information that artificially fragments the public, moving us collectively further and further from the truth. In the digital commons, facts and evidence dissolve into perspective, choice, identity. Countercultural moments become naïve, ephemeral gestures of resistance, as fleeting as the Instagram posts they generate.

```
i=d.squash(e),j=this.hash(e,i),g&&j!==d.stripHash(d.parseLocation().hash)&&(this.preventNextHashChan
c.title),f),l&&(k=new a.Event("popstate"),k.originalEvent={type:"popstate",state:null},this.squash(e,h),g||(th
.ate.isPushStateEnabled())return this.preventHashAssignPopState?(this.preventHashAssignPopState=!1
y.stack.length&&this.ignoreInitialHashChange&&(this.ignoreInitialHashChange=!1,location.href===e)?vo
ryState=f)):void this.history.direct({url:(b.originalEvent.state||{}).url||c,present:function(c,d){b.historyState
.()&&!a.event. managing digital resources and their spatial consequences ashChange)return this.preventl
t:function(c,d){b.hashchangeState=a.extend({},c),b.hashchangeState.direction=d},missing:function(){e.a
avigate.history=new a.mobile.History,a.mobile.navigate.navig visualizing environmental impacts of digita
imation:{},transition:{}},e=c.createElement("a"),f=["","webkit-","moz-","o-"];a.each(["animation","transition"],fi
r].duration=a.camelCase(d[g].prefi restructuring local governance for digital political representation ==d
=d.animation.prefix!==b,a(e).remove(),a.fn.animationComplete=function(e,f,g){var h,i,j=this,k=function(){c
tion"===l||a.support.cssAnimations&&"animation"===l?(g===b&&(a(this).context!==c&&(i=3e3*parseFlo
j).off(d[l].event,k),e.apply(j)},i),a(this).one(d[l].event,k)):a.support.cssTransitions&&"transition"===l||a.supp
=b||isNaN(i))&&(i=a.fn.animationComplete.defaultDurati reorganizing platforms through ethical codes k),
ction(a,b,c,d){function e(a){for(;a&&"undefined"!=typeof a.originalEvent;)a=a.originalEvent;return a}functi
&(g=E),f)for(l=g.length,i;l;)i=g[--l],b[i]=f[i];if(o.search(/mouse(down resisting the monopoly of the digital ii1
;if(b=a.Event(b),b.type=c,f=b.originalEvent,g=a.event.props,o.search(/^(mouse|click)/)>-1&&(g=E),f)for(l=
o=h.touches,j=h.changed.Touches,k=o&&o.length?o[0]:j&&j.length?j[0]:d))fo linking free digital pedagog
tNode}return e}function h(b,c){for(var d;b;){if(d=a.data(b,z),d&&(!c||d[c]))return b;b=b.parentNode}return
n(){G=0,k()},a.vmouse.res expanding accessible bandwidth infrastructure to the margins ino(b,c,d){var e;re
=o("v"+b.type,b),c&&(c.isDefaultPrevented()&&b.preventDefault(),c.isPropagationStopped()&&b.stopProp
==h.length&&(c=b.target,d=g(c),d.hasVirtualBinding&&(Q=P++ closing the gap in the digital divide no [0],
function s(b){if(!M){var c=e(b).touches[0],d=J,f=a.vmouse.moveDistanceThreshold,h=g(b.target);J=J||Ma
b,c,d=g(a.target);o("vmouseup",a,d),J||(b=o("vclick",a,d),b&&b.isDefaultProp designing mechanisms to de
(cin d)if(d[c])return!0;return!1}function v(){}function w(b){var c=b.substr(1);return{setup:function(){u(this)||a
art||0)+1,1===F.touchstart&&O.bind("touchstart",q).bind("touch transposing social norms of dignity and c
s).unbind("touchend",t).unbind("scroll",r));var d=a(this),e=a.data(this,z);e&&(e[b]=!1),d.unbind(c,v),u(this)||d
click vmouseout vmousecancel".split(" "),C="clientX clientY pageX pageY screenX screenY".split(" "),D=a.e
entListener"in c,O=a(c),P=1,Q=0;for(a.vmouse={moveDistanceThreshold:10,clickDistanceThreshold:10,re
,g,h,i=K.length,j=b.target;if(i)for(c=b.clientX,d=b.clientY,x=a.vmouse.clickDistanceThreshold,e=j;e;){for(f=
d b.stopPropagation();e=e.parentNode}},!0)}(a,b,c),function(a,b,d){function e(b,c,e,f){var g=e.type;e.type=
uchstart":"mousedown",j=g?"touchend":"mouseup",k=g?"touchmove":"mousemove";a.each("touchstart to
rn a?this.bind(c,a):this.trigger(c)},a.attrFn&&(a.attrFn[c]=!0)}),a.event.special.scrollstart={enabled:!0,setup
tart.enabled&&(c||b(e,!0),clearTimeout(d),d=setTimeout(function(){b(e,!1)},50))})},teardown:function. plane
vmousedown",function(g){function h(){clearTimeout(k)}function i(){h(),c.unbind("vclick",j),c.unbind("vmouse
h)return!1;vani localizing global networks for contextualizing digital injustice cancel",i),k=setTimeout(funct
shold)})},teardown:function(){a(this).unbind("vmousedown").unbind("vclick").unbind("vmouseup"),f.unbind
:30,verticalDistanceThreshold:30,getLocation:function(a){var c=b.pageXOffset,d=b.pageYOffset,e=a.clien
-=c,f-=d):(f<a.pageY-d||e<a.pageX-c)&&(e=a.pageX-c,f=a.pageY-d),{x:e,y:f}},start:function(b){var c=b.origi
s:[d.x,d.y],origin:a(b.target)}},stop:function(b){var c=b.originalEvent.touches?b.originalEvent.touches[0]:b,
me-b.time<a.event.special.swipe.durationThreshold&&Math.abs(b.coords[0]-c.coords[0])>a.event.specia
{a.addDependents(this,b)},getEncodedText:function(){return a("<a>").text(this.text()).html()},jqmEnhancea
this._getBase().set(a.mobile.path.get()),c.xhr=f,c.textStatus=g,c.errorThrown=h;var i=this._triggerWithDe
```

Reclaiming the Digital Commons

The tragedy of the digital commons is ultimately a crisis of collective will and management. While the digital commons idealizes "open access," too little attention is paid to governance, equitable access and use, and social protection. Perhaps Elinor Ostrom's classic research on common-pool resource management of fisheries, land irrigation systems, farmlands and other productive landscapes contains clues for reclaiming the digital commons today. This agenda might include such strategies as reframing the digital commons as a regional and local project with global impacts; linking analog and digital justice; creating new forms of bottom-up digital governance to promote civility, trust and cooperation, and to articulate and enforce limits on conduct to prevent discrimination and exploitation in the digital environment. These strategies might be combined with fortifying local investigative journalism, dedicated to fact-finding and pushing back against algorithmic misinformation. Local journalists can help to align abstract news cycles with life-as-lived in particular places and broker situated dialogue among diverse publics to rebuild civic trust.

shAssignPopState=!0,b.location.hash=j,this.preventHashAssignPopState=!1,h=a.extend({url:i,hash:j,title::
,a.mobile.window.trigger(k))),this.history.add(h.url,h)},popstate:function(b){var c,f;if(a.event.special.navigi
Propagation()):this.ignorePopState?void(this.ignorePopState=!1):!b.originalEvent.state&&1===this.histor
{c=d.parseLocation().hash,!b.originalEvent.state&&c?(f=this.squash(c),this.history.add(f.url,f),void(b.histoi
oryState.direction=d})))},hashchange:function(b){vare,f;if(a.event.special.navigate.isHashChangeEnabled
oid b.stopImmediatePropagation();e=this.history,f=d.parseLocation().hash,this.history.direct({url:f,presen
)}})}})}})}})(a),function(a){a.mobile.navigate=function(b,c,d){a.mobile.navigate.navigator.go(b,c,d)},a.mobile.n
consumption rseLocation();a.mobile.navigate.history.add(b.href,{hash:b.hash})}(a),function(a,b){var d={an
==c?g+"-name":g;a.each(f,function(c,f){return e.style[a.camelCase(f+h)]!==b?(d[g].prefix=f,!1):void 0)},d[g:
t=d[g].event.toLowerCase())}),a.support.cssTransitions=d.transition.prefix!==b,a.support.cssAnimationsr
y(this,arguments)},l=f&&"animation"!==f?"transition":"animation";returna.support.cssTransitions&&"transil
tion))),(0===i||i===b||isNaN(i))&&(i=a.fa challenging algorithmic discrimination =setTimeout(function(){a(i
"animation"===l?(g===b&&(a(this).context!==c&&(i=3e3*parseFloat(a(this).css(d[l].duration))),(0===i||i==
e(d[l].event,k)):(setTimeout(a.proxy(e,this),0),a(this))},a.fn.animationComplete.defaultDuration=1e3}(a),furn
m,n,o=b.type;if(b=a.Event(b),b.type=c,f=b.originalEvent,g=a.event.props,o.search(/^(mouse|click)/)>-1r&
ch/)&&(h=e(f),o=h.touches,j=h.changedTouches,k=o&&o.length?o[0]::j&&j.length?f,g,h,i,j,k,l,m,n,o=b.type
i]=f[i];if(o.search(/mouse(down|up)|click/)>-1&&!b.which&&(b.which=1),-1!==o.search(/^touch/)&&(h=e(f)r
nization ng(b){for(var c,d,e={};b;){c=a.data(b,z);for(d in c)c[d]&&(e[d]=e.hasVirtualBinding=!0);b=b.parenti
function j(){M=!0}functionk(){Q=0,K.length=0,L=!1,j()}function l(){i()}function m(){n(),G=setTimeout(functio
(c.target,b))&&(e=f(c,b),a(c.target).trigger(e)),e}function p(b){var c,d=a.data(b.target,A);L||Q&&Q===d||(syn
iatePropagationStopped()&&b.stopImmediatePropagation()))}function q(b){var c,d,f,h=e(b).touches;h&&r1
,o("vmouseover",b,d),o("vmousedown",b,d)))}function r(a){M||(J||o("vmousecancel",a,g(a.target)),J=!0,m())}
Math.abs(c.pageY-l)>f,J&&!d&&o("vmousecancel",b,h),o("vmousemove",b,h),m())}function t(a){if(!M){j()v1d
gital propaganda ,y:c.clientY),L=!0)),o("vmouseout",a,d),J=!1,m())}}function u(b){var c,d=a.data(b,z);if(d)fort
a.data(this,z);d[b]=!0,F[b]=(F[b]||0)+1,1===F[b]&&O.bind(c,p),a(this).bind(c,v),N&&(F.touchstart=(F.touchsti
ealm F[b]||O.unbind(c,p),N&&(--F.touchstart,F.touchstart||O.unbind("touchstart",q).unbind("touchmovr","tr
x,y,z="virtualMouseBindings",A="virtualTouchID",B="vmouseover vmousedown vmousemove vmouseupr
.event.mouseHooks.pro demanding the civic potential of new virtual platforms K=[],L=!1,M=!1,N="addEm.
0),y=0;y<B.length;y++)a.event.special[B[y]]=w(B[y]);N&&c.addEventListener("click",function(b){varc,d,e,f
for platform's negative externalities .abs(g.y-d)<x||a.data(e,A)===g.touchID)return b.preventDefault(),vcni
d,b):a.event.dispatch.call(b,e),e.type=g}var f=a(c),g=a.mobile.support.touch,h="touchmove scroll",i=g?"to
kap t prioritizing platforms as a common good rtscrollstop".split(" "),function(b,c){a.fn[c]=function(a){return
o(a,b){c=b,e(f,c?"scrollstart":"scrollstop",a)}var c,d,f=this,g=a(f);g.bind(h,function(e){a.event.special.scroll((
digital resources holdThreshold:750,emitTapOnTaphold:!0,setup:function(){var b=this,c=a(b),d=!1;c.bind("s
usecancel",i)}function j(a){i(),d||l!==a.target?d&&a.preventDefault():e(b,"tap",a)}if(d=!1,g.which&&1!==g.whic
.tap.emitTapOnTaphold||(d=!0),e(b,"taphold",a.Event("taphold",{target:l})),a.event.special.tap.tapholdThr[h
a.event.special.swipe={scrollSupressionThreshold:30,durationThreshold:1e3,horizontalDistanceThreshol}
l rights pageY&&Math.floor(f)>Math.floor(a.pageY)||0===a.pageX&&Math.floor(e)>Math.floor(a.pageX)?(in
originalEvent.touches[0]:b,d=a.event.special.swipe.getLocation(c);return{time:(new Date).getTime(),coor{
vipe.getLocation resisting privatizing digital collective resources d.y}]},handleSwipe:function(b,c,d,f){if(c.t
stanceThreshold&&Math.abs(b.coords[1]-c.coords[1])<a.event.special.swipe.verticalDistanceThreshold){r
a.mobi designing political and economic structures to manage digital assets held in common oveWithDel
",c);i.deprecatedEvent.isDefaultPrevented()||i.event.isDefaultPrevented()||(d.showLoadMsg&&this._show
t.special.swipe.start(b),h. experimenting with new processes and practices for digital "commoning" pecial
oords[0]-d.coords[0])>a.event.special.swipe.scrollSupressionThreshold&&b.preventDefault())},e.stop=fw
esigning new critical interfaces between *Res Publica* and *Res Communis* elete b.swipe,b.length--,0=m),v
op))}},a.each({scrollstop:"scrollstart",taphold:"tap",swipeleft:"swipe.left",swiperight:"swipe.right"},functioni
event.special.throttled:r connecting digital networks with socio-ecological networks n(){a(this)unbind("res
eout(b),b=setTimeout(f,e-d))},g=0}(a),function(a,b){function d(){var a=e();a!==f&&(f=a,l.trigger(m))}var e,f,gj
),==50,g=i>j&&i-j>k,h=n[b.orientation],in linking artificial intelligence with social and spatial justice tion,di
onchange.disabled?!1:(f=e(),void l.bind("throttledresize",d))},teardown:function(){return a.support.orientati
ler=function(a){return a.orientation=e(),b.apply(this,arguments)}}}),a.event.special.orientationchange.orier
ntHeight<1.1,d?"portrait":"landscape"},a.fn[m]=function(a){return a?this.bind(m,a):this.trigger(m)},a.attrFn&
cumentBase.hrefNoHash}).prependTo(a("head")),linkSelector:"[src], link[href], a[rel='external'], :jqmData(a
obile.path.makeUrlAbsolute(b,a.mobile.path.documentBase)},rewrite:function(b,d){var e=a.mobile.path.si
ocation(),g=a(c).attr(d);g=g.replace(f.protocol+f.doubleSlash+f.host+f.pathname,""),/^(\w+:|#|\/)/.test(g)||a

Design
Mediation

Designing Interface

Top-down and bottom-up resources and knowledges need to meet, and this requires a two-way curatorial project—in one direction: bottom-up urban activism must trickles upward to transform discriminatory top-down institutions and policies; and in the other, top-down resources must effectively reach sites of marginalization. By absorbing the creative intelligence of informal urban dynamics, the top-down can also transform its institutional norms and practices. This urban journey from the bottom-up to the top-down and back again can advance urban justice today—and this requires new urban curatorial practices capable of mediation and political representation.

27

It is Not about "What" We Represent,
but "Who" We Represent

Dr. King was a designer of political representation, a social mediator capable of facilitating radical policy transformation on behalf of the unheard. Grass-roots organizations working in the trenches of social injustice often perform in similar ways, negotiating policy transformation on behalf of underrepresented communities. In our practice we forge alliances with community-based agencies to translate bottom-up social-economic processes as we negotiate alterations of exclusionary top-down urban policy. The local agencies, community groups, and religious organizations we partner with

perform as *bottom-up city halls* for their communities. They are mediators that advocate for top-down social and urban policy transformations in response to community needs and aspirations. They represent local urgencies, organize and aggregate social-economic capabilities and lobby for resources while protecting those who need to be protected. Urban justice demands an augmented role for these mediating social actors across the city to partner in the co-production of inclusive public policy and community development.

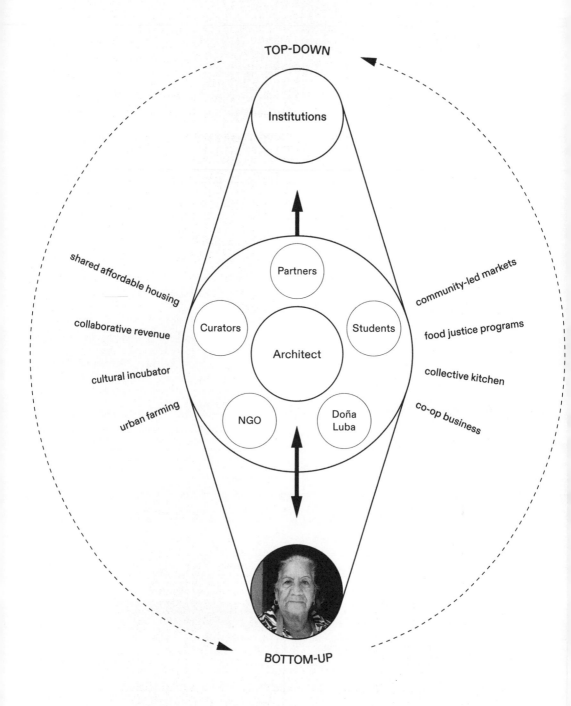

TOP-DOWN

Institutions

Partners

Curators

Architect

Students

NGO

Doña Luba

shared affordable housing

collaborative revenue

cultural incubator

urban farming

community-led markets

food justice programs

collective kitchen

co-op business

BOTTOM-UP

Designing Mediation

Bottom-up urban praxis needs institutional support and political representation, and this is a ripe space of intervention for contemporary architecture practice. Architects and urban designers can advance new curatorial practices that support underrepresented forms of labor and industry. In our practice, we have committed to co-designing socio-spatial processes of urban mediation to increase economic opportunities in migrant communities. We act as urban facilitators, linking bottom-up social actors, and the hidden value of their skills and capabilities, with top-down resources and support systems, which are often similarly inaccessible and hidden.

Doña Luba's Tamales as a Seed for Housing

1. Doña Luba is a Guatemalan immigrant who sells tamales for a living. From her tiny kitchen in a San Diego mid-city neighborhood, she generates enough business to maintain her rent and everyday necessities.

2. We met Doña Luba, loved her tamales and discussed how to scale up her informal economy. We proposed working together to develop a small housing project. We explained that while she currently does not have the financial means to participate, she has skills that can make her a partner and co-producer of a small business connected to the initiative.

3. We then engaged a local community-based NGO, which has a robust set of social service programs in the neighborhood, to discuss integrating Doña Luba's informal economy as a demonstration of increasing community capacity to develop jobs and affordable housing.

4. We partnered with the NGO to conceptualize an experimental mixed-use 6-plex housing project connected to a small economic incubator, an industrial kitchen co-owned by Doña Luba.

5. As architects we represented Doña Luba, mediating the economic and political bureaucratic processes necessary to include her. By connecting her activities to the local NGO, we proposed redirecting some initial economic support for Doña Luba in the shape of subsidies and grants.

6. We designed an economic proforma, bundling the resources of partners and their sweat equity, including the added value of Doña Luba's local food practice and her anticipated revenue. To protect Doña Luba, we helped to shape a new cooperative agency, to be managed collectively.

7. We proposed the formation of a Limited Liability Corporation to frame the partnership of all collaborators. Years ago, the local NGO had purchased the land outright. Our architect's fee (15% of construction costs) would be presented as collateral for a construction loan. The local NGO would be part of the development to engage Doña Luba's business in food-related programs and revenue. These bundled resources represent enough equity to qualify for a conventional construction loan.

8. An architect can propose to live in one of the units, qualifying for an owner-occupied loan. 2 units could be rented to MFA students from the university where we teach. One unit could become a collective Airbnb to cross-subsize student rent and facilitate food-based programs with the local NGO. One live-work unit is dedicated to Doña Luba and her industrial kitchen, and one unit generates market-rate rent.

9. Dona Luba's live-work unit faces the street. A percentage of her profit would pay her rent, making the unit affordable, while she is scaling up business operations to generate more revenue for herself as a project partner. The project illustrates that housing affordability can link with experimental sources of economic revenue as an engine of income generation.

10. The two MFA students, the local NGO and the architects can work together on special projects that feature Doña Luba's tamales, including catering food for university events and neighborhood-based cultural projects. Profits are distributed among the collaborators.

Talk to the ~~Enemy~~ Adversary

Enough Preaching to the Choir

Chances are, most of us agree on essential principles of inclusion, social justice, the urgencies of tackling climate change and the importance of promoting public thinking. But how do we engage those who don't? How do we persuade cultures of opposition? Can we better understand their logics of justification, decode the dramatic polarization of ideological, institutional, communal and familial relations? To advance social justice, we need to operate outside the safe parameters of consensus, beyond our familiar audiences, and engage those who disagree. Can we design new forms of "encounter" with the "other," to dialogue through difference, to confront mistrust and fear? Can we design new agonistic political languages that emerge from constructive contestation?

28

Border-Drain-Crossing

Over the last years, we have curated the *Political Equator Meetings*—itinerant cross-sector dialogues in the San Diego-Tijuana border region, which perform as nomadic public performances, using walking as an agonistic political practice. We negotiate with top-down institutions to gain access to contested sites of exception, adjacent and through the US-Mexico border wall, and traverse these territories with multiple stakeholders at odds with one another to recontextualize debates and conversations. In 2011, working closely with local and global actors—including community activists, scholars, artists, border patrol agents, and government leaders—we proposed to US Homeland Security and Mexican Immigration that they "re-code" an existing drain beneath the border wall into a temporary port of entry for 24 hours. This enabled our diverse convoy of 300 people to slip uninterruptedly from San Diego into Tijuana, under the jurisdictional line, to experience first-hand the impact of border wall construction on our shared environmental assets, and to expose the contradictions between national security and ecological insecurity. The *Border-Drain-Crossing* became a platform for contestation and debate, and culminated in a new mutual recognition that we need new strategies of coexistence between these divided border communities.

1. Begin with a controversy: What is the problem?

2. Summon institutions at odds with one another: gather actors representing different agencies.

5. Choreograph a script, researching a common language, mediating private, public and community sensibilities.

6. Build mediating tools to facilitate debate, finding evidence to frame the problem.

9. Situate public space as forum inside site of conflict, a stage for opening debate about institutional agendas that produce the problem.

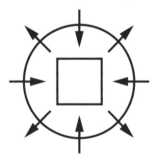

10. Rehearse how to approach consensus on overlapping interests through disagreements: play with contradictions: What if this policy does this, instead of that?

BUILDING BLOCK

An Architecture of Dialogue

Chantal Mouffe explains that power profits from consensus and justice necessitates contestation.[12] This is why "agonistic" political practices are essential today—to disrupt the smooth functioning of unjust power. Can we design the agonistic interventions in public domain? Anticipate the architecture of dialogue, protocols for debate? What tools can be helpful to visualize and mediate conflict? Can peripheral, liminal and contested sites become a new kind of open-air public forum for debate, making visible to all involved the operations of unjust power?

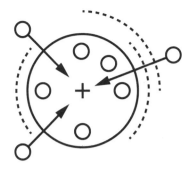

3. Develop a protocol of listening and new channels of communication.

4. Speculate on the structure of the argument to negotiate with the "other."

7. Anticipate economic, environmental and social externalities, anticipating and quantifying future impacts and consequences from current harmful policies, and their effects on individual and collective interests.

8. Engage the site of conflict as a context for conversation, where the drama of the issue can be experienced.

11. Participants as witnesses and participants: human rights are not entitlements handed down from above, but must be lived and performed from below.

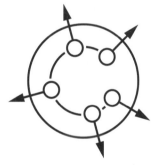

12. Use public reenactments and performances as experiential tools for accessing complexity. Institutions and communities cannot tackle the problem without experiencing it, without "seeing" it, without meeting and listening to those who are most affected.

Problematize "Sustainability"

Sustainability Begins with Civically Engaged Publics

Climate change is the existential challenge of our time. Although we are all at risk, under-served communities of color are uniquely vulnerable and least capable of adapting to the impacts of climate change. Climate justice demands that those who cause harm, especially those who benefit from it, bear primary responsibility both to remediate the suffering of populations struggling to adapt, and also to mitigate future harm by doing everything we now know is necessary to mobilize a low-carbon global economy, including helping developing populations leap-frog what got us into trouble, and tempering the promotion of our sprawling development and wasteful lifestyle as the epitome of human happiness. The issue is urgent, and intensifying with each passing day. In the US, the *Green New Deal* has emerged as a strategy for tackling climate change while growing jobs and strengthening our economy. However, the "green" part of the equation gets far more attention than the New Deal dimension, which we believe is necessary to achieve the *green*. Climate change represents a dramatic failure of public will and political leadership. We speak in urban design circles about "sustainability"—but this demands civically engaged publics who believe in public goods and social equity, who understand that the well-being of the individual rests on the well-being of the community, and who demand that we redistribute collective resources to eliminate carbon emission and accelerate adaptation efforts in vulnerable communities.

29

Sustainable Hummer?

Urban growth patterns across the world endorse a super-size-me, car-centric, oil-based lifestyle. Urban planning and design tends to approach the climate crisis through the rubric of "sustainability," and the retrofitting of our cities and infrastructure with climate friendly policies and technologies. But it is ultimately irrelevant whether buildings are wrapped with smart green envelopes or photovoltaic solar panels if all these approaches become a symbolic check-list to camouflage a selfish way of life and a refusal to alter social priorities, norms and behaviors. When we assembled the image below, we never imagined (but should have!) that Hummer would soon produce an EV line. Without reclaiming a commitment to public goods, without recognizing that we are all on this ship together, without revising the policies and economic models that have perpetuated urban growth on steroids, sustainability will remain a rhetorical trope, a developer's PR campaign to evade hard questions and solutions.

It is not only about polar bears

It is about people, and especially the most vulnerable among us.
It is about elevating adaptation along with mitigation. People are hurting!
It is about localizing climate literacy and climate justice in the everyday life of people.

It is not only about carrots

It is about sticks, public institutions committed to the public good.
It is about political leadership.
It is about an informed voting public.

It is not only about technology innovation

It is about changing hearts and minds through climate education.
It is about bottom-up, participatory climate action.
It is about proactive top-down energy policy.

It is not only about LEED checklists

It is about denouncing sprawl, horizontally and vertically.
It is about challenging uneven urban growth.
It is about neighborhood-scale social and economic sustainability.

It is not only about profit

It is about innovating affordable energy provision for the public good.
It is about public science and community-based innovations that improve peoples' lives.
It is about universities committing to "technology transfer for social justice."

It is not only about "applying" technologies to communities

It is about distributed energy systems that connect individual savings to community benefits.
It is about incentivizing local innovation and economy.
It is about accelerating STEAM learning and access to higher education.

BUILDING BLOCK

Bending the Curve

The *Bending the Curve Report* (2015) was written by fifty University of California researchers across disciplines to highlight the integral strategies that have made California a living laboratory for climate change solutions—from policy and technology to finance and land-use, to social norms and behavioral change. It was led by climate scientist Veerabhadran Ramanathan (UC San Diego), political theorist Fonna Forman (UC San Diego) and energy policy researcher Daniel Kammen (UC Berkeley).[10]

Climate change is too often reduced to a "scientific" problem to be solved by "technological" innovations. But as we invent new technologies and design progressive climate policy, we also need to update our social technologies, how we communicate about climate change, particularly to resistant and apathetic publics. It is a mistake to see this subject as window dressing to hard-nosed scientific thinking about climate solutions. Broad climate literacy is essential to saving millions of tons of carbon in the US and across the world in the coming years.

Additionally, as a matter of climate justice, we urgently need to accelerate adaptation strategies in partnership with vulnerable communities—bending the curve of climate vulnerability as we bend the curve of global warming, adapting as we mitigate.

Climate Justice Redistributes Global Responsibilities for the Common Good

Rethinking urban and social justice through climate.
Linking environmental and social justice: "the cry of the earth, the cry of the poor."
Climate justice links human rights and urban-community development.

1. Go Local	2. Understand Impacts	3. End with Action
Addressing Harms		**Community Strategies**

Intragenerational harms: Addressing the disproportionate impacts of climate change on vulnerable groups in our generation.	**Adaptation Strategies:** Increasing community capacity to adapt to a changing climate.
Intergenerational harms: Addressing the disproportionate impacts of climate change on future generations, those not yet born.	**Mitigation Strategies:** Increasing community capacity to participate in climate action.

Bending the Curve: *Ten Solutions*

1. Bend the warming curve immediately by reducing short-lived climate pollutants (SLCPs) and going fossil-free.	2. Foster a global culture of climate action through coordinated public communication and education at local to global scales. Combine technology and policy solutions with innovative approaches to changing social attitudes and behavior.
3. Deepen the global culture of climate collaboration. Design venues where stakeholders, community and religious leaders converge around concrete problems with researchers and scholars from all academic disciplines, with the overall goal of initiating collaborative actions to mitigate climate disruption.	4. Scale subnational models of governance and collaboration around the world to embolden and energize national and international action.
5. Adopt market-based instruments to create efficient incentives for businesses and individuals to reduce CO_2 emissions.	6. Narrowly target direct regulatory measures, such as rebates and efficiency and renewable energy portfolio standards, at high emissions sectors not covered by market-based policies.
7. Promote immediate widespread use of mature technologies such as photovoltaics, wind turbines, battery and hydrogen fuel cell electric light-duty vehicles and more efficient end-use devices, especially in lighting, air-conditioning, appliances and industrial processes.	8. Aggressively promote innovations to accelerate the complete electrification of energy and transportation systems and improve building efficiency.
9. Immediately make maximum use of available technologies combined with regulations to reduce methane emissions by 50 percent and black carbon emissions by 90 percent. Phase out hydrofluorocarbons (HFCs) by 2030 by amending the Montreal Protocol.	10. Regenerate damaged natural ecosystems and improve natural sinks for carbon (through restoration of soil organic carbon, reforestation, and dramatically reducing deforestation.)

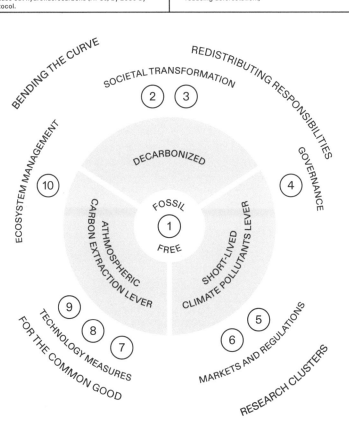

BUILDING BLOCKS

Retool Ourselves

Intervening in Our Own Practices

We end where we began, coming full circle to the imperative of self-critique. We are at a critical juncture in history defined by unprecedented crises that call into question traditional methods of artistic and architectural intervention in the city, urban scholarship and research. Meeting the moment demands an examination of our assumptions, our motivations and our ways of thinking and making as architects and designers. Normative design protocols require us to intervene in sites and conditions outside ourselves, but today's crises will require us to look inward, seeing our own methods as fertile zones for scrutiny and self-reflection, transforming our own practices into the most important site of intervention and experimentation. In other words, reclaiming the emancipatory role of architecture as a social medium is made possible through a sense of urgency, pushing us to rethink our procedures, expand our modes of artistic practice, and seek alternative sites of research and pedagogy. Facing a world of impossible challenges, we must ultimately become impossibly comprehensive, complicating our processes by seeking and intersecting with a wider set of priorities, expanding our checklist, not only to solve problems but to frame them more critically.

30

Diagramming Practice: 5Ws + HOW

For years, our work has focused on marginalized zones across the San Diego-Tijuana border region. Building an embedded practice committed to this geography of conflict and disparity has meant being very deliberate about our priorities: Why, for whom, and where do we want to build, and why? And when will we not build? These questions yield an operative diagram of the conflicts invisibly embedded in such locations, as the basis for our design process.

WHY do we do what WHAT we do? For WHOM? WHERE? WHEN? and HOW? We begin to address these questions by constructing a table that lists the 5Ws, followed by a relational map that visualizes the multiple vectors of exclusionary force and their intersectional compounding impacts (economic, social, political, cultural and environmental) on the local communities that inhabit these low-income neighborhoods. We conclude with speculative strategies to tackle them—what we call the HOW. This is the *Practice Diagram*, our machine for provocations and controversies, a discursive platform that provokes critique and revision of our own methods for intervention, identifying zones of weakness and vulnerability in our practice, and the detours we must take to engage domains conventionally peripheral to design, but essential for social transformation.

BUILDING BLOCKS

WHERE	01

WHERE is the space, site, zone, geography of investigation and potential intervention. Narrativize the conditions, the context. As much as this has to do with physical place, it also has to do with non-place. WHERE must engage the geography itself, but also, more critically, the power dynamics inscribed in that geography: the allegorical and metaphorical meanings (and for whom), the institutional entanglements, the regulatory frameworks, the jurisdictional designations, the economic interests, the cultural meanings, and networks of control. What are the visible and invisible conditions that constitute the location—conceptual, material, infrastructural, environmental, institutional, political, jurisdictional, regulatory, economic, historical, cultural and social forces that define the territory and the objects it contains?

WHY	02

WHY pertains to the critical issues, questions, challenges, conflicts, controversies, provocations, violations, injustices and indignities that arise in your case study, sometimes visibly, sometimes invisibly. WHY motivates your urban / architectural proposition. WHY do you care? WHY should others care? WHY will you propose what you propose? And WHY should others support it? WHY refers to the issues of concern—political, ethical, social, cultural, economic, environmental—embedded in your case, the fire behind your investigation and urban / architectural proposition.

WHAT	03

WHAT refers to the impacts of the WHY, on real people, on communities, on the environment, on the public. If the WHY is racial injustice, for example, the WHAT refers to the impacts of this: perhaps higher rates of disease and mortality, poorly funded schools, neighborhood divestment, decay, abandoned buildings, homelessness, gentrification, perhaps despair, loss of hope. The WHAT is your evidence of the WHY. The WHAT is the causal output or detritus of the WHY that animates your interest in the case study, and the possible urban / architectural interventions you will propose. The WHAT can be about visible material things, objects, but also about invisible ephemeral, emotional or aspirational things.

WHO	04

WHO pertains to the people and groups invested in the site, who are impacted by its evolution over time, who have capacities to alter the conditions, and who are the potential audiences of your proposal. WHO is harmed and WHO benefits from the status quo, and from a change in the status quo? WHO must be negotiated with, exchanged with, persuaded, infiltrated? WHO are the institutions you must "deal" with, learn from, utilize, disrupt, encroach into? WHO must be engaged in any potential proposition? There may be people / institutions / stakeholders that don't yet exist. Sometimes WHO needs to be imagined, narrativized, designed, created, incubated, choreographed, manipulated. Remember too that we as architects and urbanists are part of the WHO: How can we identify, understand, translate, communicate, narrativize, visualize, represent the impacts, if we are newcomers to the contested site? WHO is best situated to represent the WHAT? WHO narrates the city?

WHEN	05

WHEN pertains to the temporal dimensions of the condition—the histories, sequences, durations, rhythms, processes, that constitute the condition and must drive any potential urban / architectural proposition. Characteristics of slow, "laggy," early, late, rapid, urgent, regressive, progressive, incremental and gradual, anticipatory, innovative, reactionary, revolutionary are all examples of temporal descriptors. The temporalization of space is necessary to understand the WHY and ultimately to manifest your vision.

HOW: Practice Diagram	06

What emerges from the 5Ws is a narrative that exposes the vectors and forces that are play in a site of conflict. These vectors become the building blocks, the materials for the HOW: The Conflict Diagram. This is a "scaffold for things to happen," a generative tool for proposition that is rooted in the contingencies and opportunities of a contested zone. A Conflict Diagram is an anticipatory framework that sets up the controversies, opportunities and creative possibilities for urban, architectural and political intervention. Conflict Diagrams advance the notion that designing political, social and economic processes is the prerequisite to urbanizations and architectures of social justice.

BUILDING BLOCK

The Practice Diagram

As architects we typically wait for the client and the brief in order to design within a given site and budget. The Practice Diagram is our tool to design the brief and the client—an urban script for engaging the stakeholders and insititutions, the political, social and economic processes that are necessary to spatialize justice; to summon all the materials necessary to take a political stance, to advocate for more equitable, sustainable and civically relevant spatial interventions, and to co-produce the city with others. The Practice Diagram mediates the interface between the top-down and the bottom-up.

TOP-DOWN RESOURCES

supporting bottom-up intelligence

THE CHALLENGES OF CONTEMPORARY URBANIZATION

deepening social-economic inequality | dramatic migratory shifts | informal urbanization
climate change | thickening of borders | erosion of public thinking

EXPOSING CONFLICT AS OPERATIONAL TOOL

the visualization of political and civic process

POLITICAL ECONOMY ◄——► POLITICAL JURISDICTION

who owns the resources?   whose territory is it?

FRAGMENTED INSTITUTIONS

POLICIES ◄—— KNOWLEDGES ——► RESOURCES

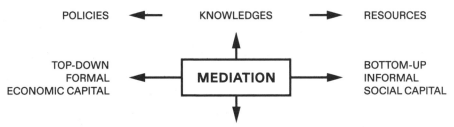

TOP-DOWN
FORMAL
ECONOMIC CAPITAL ◄—— **MEDIATION** ——► BOTTOM-UP
INFORMAL
SOCIAL CAPITAL

CURATING COLLABORATION AND REDISTRIBUTION OF KNOWLEDGES & RESOURCES

EXPANDED MODEL OF PRACTICE

designing the interface

ECONOMIC PROFORMAS ◄—— POLICY FRAMEWORKS ——► SPATIAL JUSTICE

community is a   density measures social   infrastructure spatializes
developer   exchanges per area   inclusion

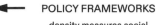

TACTICS OF TRANSLATION

economic solidarity | social resilience | adaptive urbanization
empathy as political tool | shared jurisdiction | civic imagination

transforming top-down policy

BOTTOM-UP INTELLIGENCE

BUILDING BLOCKS